The Thin Black Line

Hugh Holton
The Thin Black Line

True Stories by Black Law
Enforcement Officers Policing
America's Meanest Streets

**A Tom Doherty
Associates Book
New York**

THE THIN BLACK LINE: TRUE STORIES BY BLACK LAW ENFORCEMENT
OFFICERS POLICING AMERICA'S MEANEST STREETS

Copyright © 2008 by Elizabeth Cook and Ed Gorman

A Forge Book
Published by Tom Doherty Associates, LLC
175 Fifth Avenue
New York, NY 10010

www.tor-forge.com

Forge® is a registered trademark of Tom Doherty Associates, LLC.

Library of Congress Cataloging-in-Publication Data

Holton, Hugh.
The thin black line : true stories by black law enforcement officers policing
America's meanest streets / Hugh Holton.—1st ed.
        p.   cm.
    "A Tom Doherty Associates Book."
    ISBN-13: 978-0-312-86820-8
    ISBN-10: 0-312-86820-0
    1. Police—United States—Case studies.   2. Law enforcement—United
States—Case studies.   I. Title.
HV8139 .H65 2009
363.2'308996073—dc22

                                                                2008038109

First Edition: January 2009

Printed in the United States of America

0 9 8 7 6 5 4 3 2 1

Contents

Contents

Editor's Note

While I was editing *The Thin Black Line,* I mentioned to Hugh Holton that I had asked several of the cops in the book about race discrimination in police departments and that few of them wanted to discuss it, let alone put it in the book.

I knew Hugh extremely well, and he never really discussed it either.

I grew up in a town not far from Hugh, and we were the same age. I mentioned that I knew something about police racism in our region. Among other things, when Hugh and I were growing up in the 1950s and '60s, most police departments—city and state—had strict racial quotas. Hugh had clearly experienced these sorts of things. Hugh, however, never complained about racism. The one time I pressed him on the subject, he implied to me that dwelling on such things was counterproductive for him personally.

Surprisingly few of the officers whom I talked to in this book wanted to discuss it.

The one time I pressed Hugh on the subject, he related an incident that he said he would not put in the book: He was still a very active police officer, and he honestly loved the Chicago PD. He did say, however, that he wanted to write about the incident one day.

One of the problems with predeceasing your editor is that the editor gets a larger say in determining the book's content. Since Hugh did ultimately want to write about that incident, I will relate the incident for him. It concerns how Hugh got on the Chicago police force.

Hugh was a Vietnam combat veteran. After he got back from Vietnam, he applied to the Chicago Police Department. When he took his physical, he was one of seventeen black applicants. Sixteen out of the seventeen candidates were rejected for flat feet and heart arrhythmias—ailments that were measured subjectively and largely undemonstrable—and Hugh was one of those rejected.

Hugh went home, put on his Vietnam uniform, and returned to apply for a second physical. He explained to the sergeant that if he was healthy enough for Vietnam combat, he was healthy enough for the Chicago PD. One of the cops overseeing the physicals said, "Hell, Hugh, I didn't know you were a Vietnam vet. Forget about it. You passed."

I told that story to a very tough, very impressive black police chief, who contributed a piece for this book. I expected outrage. Instead, his face saddened, and his eyes almost teared.

"Think of all the wasted opportunities out there," he said. "Think of all the wasted talent."

Like Hugh, the people in this book are astonishingly strong.

Like Hugh, they are all genuine heroes.

ROBERT GLEASON
Executive Editor
Forge Books

Prologue

African-Americans have served in police-related functions in America since before the Revolutionary War. But the first documented instance of a "free man of color" working as an officer on an organized police force was in New Orleans in 1805. Black officers served throughout the antebellum South as slave catchers and during the Reconstruction era to enforce laws exclusively against recently freed slaves. Such officers were few in number; they served under the supervision of whites and were prohibited from enforcing the law against Caucasians. As Reconstruction gave way to Jim Crow politics in the South, African-Americans were excluded from police work to the extent of almost total elimination until the advent of the Civil Rights Movement of the mid-1950s.

In Chicago the first black officer was appointed in 1872, which was to date the first appointment of an African-American to a law enforcement agency outside the South. Blacks did comparatively well in Chicago between 1872 and 1930, accounting for more officers than was the case in any other American city with the exception of Philadelphia. From the 1930s through the 1960s, African-Americans were appointed to northern police forces based more on political patronage than merit, and their numbers were severely limited in the ranks due to bias in hiring and promotions.

The violence that erupted in major cities across the nation in the wake of the assassination of Dr. Martin Luther King Jr. in April 1968 caused the law enforcement hierarchy at all levels to rethink its policies regarding the hiring of minority officers. Even in the highly segregated South, the value of having blacks police African-American neighborhoods was realized despite the fact that upward mobility was extremely limited due to discrimination. In the 1970s, these promotion practices were challenged in federal court, leading to black officers rising through the ranks to occupy supervisory and command positions in police departments throughout the nation. At the dawn of the twenty-first century there are a number of African-Americans occupying the top slots in such major American cities as Chicago, Los Angeles, and Washington, D.C.

Over the last ten years, American policing has been rocked by horrendous scandals, from the racism of an L.A. detective investigating the murder charges against O. J. Simpson to the deviant sexual assault of an unarmed Haitian immigrant prisoner by a New York police officer. In Chicago, high-ranking police officers, including a former superintendent, have been linked to organized-crime figures and homicide cover-ups, and have come under indictment for involvement in mob-connected million-dollar jewelry robberies.

It cannot be disputed that the actions of law enforcement officers are of great interest to the public, and justifiably so. In a democratic society we must keep a watchful eye on those invested with the powers of arrest. But perhaps too often we are drawn as a society to the headline stories and newscasts narrating the sordid details of another police scandal, while merely glancing at or ignoring the "cop slain" story, which appears far more often than the "cop scandal."

As is the case in any profession, there are good cops and there are bad cops. But, due to public scrutiny, which includes numerous media offerings from motion pictures to novels with varying degrees of quality and accuracy, the police are constantly in the spotlight. However, seldom is any attempt made to truly understand the cop. To come to the realization that he or she did not arrive on earth in a rocket ship and emerge wrapped in a blue police uniform of invincibility. That cops are all too human and, in the vast majority of cases, come from the same jurisdictions that they serve in. That they have faults, which the misconduct scandals will attest to, and that they bleed red blood, which the number of officers killed and wounded each year in this country will testify to.

The Thin Black Line relates the tales of African-American officers in their own words. This volume is in no way meant to imply that these officers are any better or more qualified than any of their white, Hispanic, or other colleagues. But it cannot be denied that these "people of color" have a unique heritage dating back to that first documented black officer who served in the New Orleans Police Department back in 1805. These stories are told in their own voices, relating the events leading up to their joining their respective agencies (many were simply looking for a good job with a secure pension), and they will also tell of their lives prior to joining the force. In some cases, their life stories are as fascinating as their police careers, such as the Chicago police commander who served in Casablanca in North Africa during World War II. There are two things that they all have in common: Each of them is proud to be a law enforcement officer, and they all are credits to their profession. And as much as the names Fuhrman, Volpe, and Perez have brought discredit to the law enforcement profession in recent years, the officers in *The Thin Black Line* will show the high level of commitment that they have to the profession, which will enable them to serve as role models for generations of police officers to come.

HUGH HOLTON

The Thin Black Line

Deputy Sergeant Winroe Reed (retired)

LaPorte County, Indiana, Sheriff's Department

Winroe Reed is a retired sergeant in the LaPorte County, Indiana, Sheriff's Department. He is six feet tall and weighs two hundred pounds, and a longtime friend of Sergeant Reed said that as a young man he was an extraordinary athlete and utterly fearless. He also remembers Reed as having "a burning sense of justice." Those same traits have obviously followed him through his law enforcement career.

I worked for the LaPorte County Sheriff's Department for thirty-one years—from 1968 through 1999. Much of my work involved "serving arrest warrants," which means arresting people. When people are charged with a crime in LaPorte County, someone has to go after them—assuming they haven't turned themselves in voluntarily—even if they leave the jurisdiction. Frequently that someone was me.

For decades I traveled the country serving warrants, but most of my work was done in the Indiana area—including Illinois and Michigan. I made many trips to the slums of Gary, Indiana, and the Cook County lockup in Chicago, which are pretty rough places. In other words, I've had to bring in some very tough guys—often single-handedly.

When I drove out to serve a warrant, I usually kept five sets of waist-wrist shackles and five sets of leg irons in the trunk. By nature I'm a nice guy and try hard to be respectful to the people I pick up. However, sometimes these people are just plain nasty. Not only do they have nasty mouths, even if they are shackled, they may well try to bite, butt, or rear back and kick you. The really violent people, I've been known to shackle with multiple sets of irons—legs and wrists. I tell these people in advance that I'm a kind man, but don't mistake kindness for weakness.

I don't know how many people I've brought to justice over a thirty-one-year career. Thousands, I would guess. I remember one guy lived right on the Indiana–Michigan border, and he was hard to catch. He was not only brutal, he had some "rabbit" in him. The first time I went after him, I was alone, and when I couldn't cover both doors, he skipped out the back door and bolted across the state line. Later I spotted him laughing at me from the safety of Michigan, where I was not authorized to follow and arrest him.

Then he ran off.

I had quite a problem apprehending him and had to make several attempts. One time I let the air out of his tires so he couldn't jump in his car and split. I was persistent, though. I finally staked his house out from down the street and saw him sneak back home.

He wasn't laughing when I caught him.

A lot of newspapers call Gary, Indiana—in Lake County—some pretty bad things, such as "the Homicide Capital of the United States," and it does have an unusually high murder rate, frequently the highest in the country. As you can imagine, it's not always easy to get officers to go in there and arrest people. I've had to serve a lot of arrest warrants in Gary all by myself. Usually I would stop off at the local precinct to let them know that the LaPorte County Sheriff's Department was in town and to ask if any of them wanted to keep me company. The answer was invariably, "No!"

Once I remember I had to go in alone and bring back a six-foot-nine-inch crack-addicted murderer. He was much feared and extremely violent. Now, a guy that big and wild isn't exactly inconspicuous. Still, he'd been at large for a while. I don't think anyone else wanted to go in and get him.

During most arrests you aren't supposed to knock on the door with your gun drawn. Some people will never see past the gun, will bolt or pull a gun themselves. When I suspected the guy was homicidal—if he had a really violent rap sheet, for instance—I would have the warrant on a clipboard, which I held in front of my stomach, upright. But behind the clipboard I kept a pistol.

More than once the suspect would pull a gun, only to see me drop the clipboard and put my own piece on him. Which was how I apprehended the six-foot-nine-inch crack-addict killer.

One of the weirder warrants I served was on a guy who had a wicked temper and a bad history of violence. He also had two terrifying dogs—a rottweiler and a pit bull. He also owned a lot of guns and threatened his neighbors routinely. He had a rap sheet. We had complaints on him and finally someone had him charged. It wasn't enough to send him to prison, but it was enough to arrest him.

The dogs had also terrorized the neighborhood, so before I went over there, I put on my Kevlar vest, cartridge bandoleers, multiple cartridge belts, pepper mace, extra clips, extra cuffs, and several sidearms. When I knocked, his wife answered the door.

"I have to serve this warrant on your husband and take him in," I said. "Now, I know you have two dogs, and you don't want them hurt. So I'm going to give you two hours to put them up someplace. Because when I come back, if they attack, I'll shoot them."

When I came back two hours later, the family had moved out, which satisfied the terrified neighbors.

I was on the department marksmanship team and in fact helped to train the other members. I traveled with them around the state for eight or nine years, shooting against other teams in marksmanship contests. A perfect score was 300. I got so many 300s in a row that the judges asked me to step out and shoot by myself so they could watch. They didn't think anyone could run up that many consecutive perfect scores. They thought I was scamming them.

Pretty soon, several of our guys began shooting consecutive 300s. We were beating everybody in the state, so they doubled the number of shots both sides had to take, and I once scored 599 out of 600.

Even though I'm retired I still instruct firearms at the police academy. I teach them all the basics, including how to center their sights, how to be comfortable with their firearm and not flinch. To that end I have them dry-fire their guns first, then fire one round, after which they continue dry-firing. I've helped to produce some superb students.

Sometimes people ask if I'm happy in retirement. I answer, yes. I head up security at a local hospital, which is both interesting and challenging. You have a lot of wonderful people doing fine work in hospitals, but you also have drugs, vulnerable patients, agitated visitors, and occasionally unsavory people walk in. Hospital security requires a lot of tact, intelligence, and diplomacy. Another reason I enjoy retirement is that I don't have to go into high-crime areas anymore and serve arrest warrants. I was afraid if I continued doing that, I'd shoot somebody.

Or somebody would shoot me.

LaVerne Dunlap (retired)

Police Officer

LaVerne Dunlap is a retired police officer in a steel town just north of Gary, Indiana. Like Gary—the so-called Homicide Capital of the United States—her city has a high crime rate. LaVerne Marie Dunlap was a police officer in her city for more than thirty years and was one of the first women police officers hired in that area. Attractive, with an outrageous sense of humor and an infectious laugh, she worked undercover throughout northern Indiana.

I joined the police force for two reasons. Police work appealed to me. When I first got out of school, it was 1965. I considered police work, but they were only hiring meter maids then. Then, in '69 I was on a road trip with a band in Mississippi. We were staying in a motel when a cop showed up one night. He dragged us out of our room and took us down to jail. He locked us up because we'd gone swimming in the motel pool.

I swore that if I ever became a cop I would put a stop to that kind of injustice.

After getting out of that mess and returning home, two ministers and the head of the local NAACP approached me in 1971. They said the city was now hiring policewomen. They wanted black women on the force, and they wondered if I would like to apply. They thought I would do a good job for the black community and represent our people well. As I said, police work appealed to me, but I also kept thinking, Yeah, I see some racist stuff going down, I can flash my badge and make it right—so that the stuff that happened to me in Mississippi wouldn't happen to other people. I liked helping people, too, and understood that a cop has that opportunity as well. After a few weeks on the force, however, my desire to help people eclipsed everything else. When I saw what happened to people, I really hoped I could do some good.

When the department hired me, I became the second black policewoman on the force—not counting meter maids. My friend Dottie was the first. Just because they hired my partner and me, however, didn't mean they knew what to do with us. The police force didn't even have uniforms for us and didn't know where to put us.

It was interesting being on the police department and having to bridge all those gaps, race and gender both. It was exciting, too—being new on the force, walking up and down the dark streets. You're young, and you don't think of the dangers.

Eventually the force put us on the tact squad, posing as street whores. On one of my first busts a man comes yelling at me, "Hey, sister, get off the street. We just robbed that guy, and the cops gonna show up."

When we worked undercover on the street, one of the black-and-whites would try to stay nearby, so when I went around the corner—out of sight of the hold-up guy—I spotted it pretty quick. I jumped up and down, waving at it. After I told them what happened, cop cars swarmed the guys with sirens blaring and cherries flashing. When the mugger saw us talking to the cops and all friendly with them, he started yelling at me, "What'd you do? What'd you do?" He didn't know we were cops but suspected we'd snitched him out.

One of my former police chiefs, Barry Nothstine, still laughs at one of the things that happened to me. One night we had alarms going off at the municipal golf course. The gate was locked. No one was in attendance, so I had to scale the fence. While I'm climbing the fence, I got caught—I mean really stuck. The other cops had to find a way into maintenance and bring me a stepladder.

I got stuck in a window once with my butt sticking out. Barry gets a laugh out of that one, too.

I worked undercover with Dottie in South Bend for one year on the drug squad. Again, we posed as streetwalkers with big Afro wigs.

At night we ran into some scary shit out there. We'd have to climb dark steps, buying drugs.

One night I was working with Sue, who's white but who was wearing this black Afro wig. I was wearing these little hot pants. We're there to buy drugs, but then this guy comes out of a house and jumps in the car. I knew who he was. He was a very tough, very violent criminal, who'd just gotten out of prison for shooting a man. This guy's armed, crazy, and looking like he might rob us. Sue and I are undercover, building cases. We don't want to blow our covers but don't want to get robbed or killed either. I'm thinking, Where's our backup? Meanwhile, the guy in the backseat's lookin' scary.

Just about that time, a cop car comes roaring up the street— lights flashing, the siren blaring. Two officers in a black-and-white are pulling Sue and me out of the car and searching us. They allow this guy to slip out of the car and run off down the street.

Working undercover out of town in places like Gary and South Bend is scary as hell. Going after some of the major drug dealers and hearing they were looking for me also had me hearing footsteps. Having to go out of town to testify in court—accompanied by four armed guards, never traveling in the same car, never traveling by the same route—those are the sorts of things that kept me up nights. The court trips were so dangerous, in fact, the judge would keep everyone in court until I was well out of there.

People can't tell me, my sister, and my cousin apart, and when men came gunning for me, I feared for them. Even years later stuff would happen. One time we were in a nightclub called Bob's. We were up there one night, and this guy starts threatening me. Luckily I was with several South Bend cops.

In another place, some guys started leaning on me over a bust I'd made years before, and I had to pull out my piece. I backed them up against a wall and got the hell out of the place. That was creepy, too.

One of the worst things happened when was I about to get out of a car and enter an apartment complex. Someone fired a shot and hit a car window as I was leaving the car. There was an open apartment window, and when we searched the apartment, we found shell casings on the floor.

After a while, though, your anger takes over and you aren't afraid. You just want to tear into someone.

I love police work. I've done everything. I've gone diving in Lake Michigan for bodies and evidence with the dive team. In fact, the first time I went out, our team brought a body up. I wanted to be a motorcycle cop at one time, and I had to take a lot of tests to qualify. They were heavy bikes, and I had a big Harley, which I was expected to ride. I had to lay it down and pick it up. The Harley was so heavy, I had to get my hip into it. One of my friends baited and teased me so hard—saying I would never do it—that when my turn came, I picked that bike up so fast and so furiously it bounced.

Car chases were exciting, but bike chases were even more exhilarating.

My greatest day was when they passed the wife- and child-battery law. That meant you could bust down the door if the batterer didn't let you in and that you could use all necessary force if you believed the victim's life was in mortal peril.

When I came on, I had to make a lot of collars by myself—in part because the older cops wanted to find out if the young cops could do their job. I was alone one night—shortly after the battery law was passed—but I still think I brought in seven wife batterers that first night single-handed.

I was especially anxious to bring them in when the men were beating on their wives, girlfriends, and on children. One guy I brought in, I had to kick his door down to get to him. He had his wife on the floor, and he was kneeling over her, hammering her face with his fists. He wouldn't stop beating her. I grabbed his shoulder, shouted at him to stop, identified myself as a police officer, and yanked back on his shoulder. None of it did any good. Instead of stopping, he glared back at me, shouting, "Get your hands off me, you fucking black bitch!"

All the while he kept on hitting her.

I was already mad at him for beating that poor girl. Her face was battered and bloody, and for all I knew he was inflicting brain damage. He was also a big man, clearly out of control, and I was alone. He'd been hitting her a long time and could have even killed that woman in front of me, the way he was going.

I also hated it when men called me "a fucking black bitch," and you can't imagine how many times I heard that from wife beaters when I'd interrupt their fun.

She was in mortal peril, I was all alone, and under the law I could use all necessary force. We carried these big long Maglites. I had to whale on his back and shoulders with it to make him stop. Then I had to drag him to his feet. I expected him to attack me when I got him on his feet, and I had that Maglite in my right fist. When he rushed me, he was screaming, "You fucking black bitch!" over and over.

I leaned back one step, letting him think he had me. I slipped a punch, then swung the Maglite at him two-handed. I laid it upside his head like a Louisville Slugger.

A lot of nights I banged on the door of another guy who was a compulsive batterer. He'd beat up both his wife and kids, and the neighbors would call the cops. First time I went through his door—after they passed the wife- and child-battery law—he also wouldn't stop beating on them. He also kept calling me "a fucking black bitch," and when he attacked me, he got the Maglite, too—that time between the eyes.

One night I had this guy stalking me in his car. He'd follow me everywhere I drove. I guess he was drunk out of his mind and trying to get my attention. Sometimes he'd pass me, then try to run me off the road, then fall back and tailgate me some more. I was alone. I could have called for assistance, but I was determined to handle it myself.

Finally, he passed me one last time. I tried to pull him over, but he wouldn't pull over. So I *ran* him off the road, and he flipped his car. Some officers came on the scene, dragged him out of the car, and he still came after me. I had to use my Maglite to stop him.

He was so drunk the next morning he had a blackout. When he got to court, he told the judge he couldn't remember anything. Still, he pointed at me and said, "I don't know what happened, Your Honor, but that black bitch there, you gotta *fire* her black ass!"

Now, I'm a woman, and I've had to handle some pretty tough men by myself, and sometimes I had to fight them hand-to-hand even though they outweighed me over two to one. One technique I employed was to get two fingers into their nose. That would take the fight out of most men. Once in the local jail, though, I tried to restrain a guy in the cell block. He swung on me, I got my fingers in his nose, and he didn't care. He fought so hard he drove my fingernails through his nostrils.

In the end, you try not to think about the scary things. You focus instinctively on the comic stuff. I remember once the dispatcher sent my partner and me to a domestic disturbance. My partner had the wife in one room, and I was talking to the husband in another. I had my back to the open door and thought my partner had the wife under control. It was one of those nights. Something told me to turn around. Luckily, I did, or I'd be dead. The wife had broken free from my partner and was charging me with a butcher knife in her fist. She would have stabbed me if I hadn't turned around and drawn my gun. Also her kids were screaming, "No, Mama, no." Her kids also got her to stop.

We got called once on New Year's Eve to a suicide. A man had shot himself in the head. We enter his house, and he's sitting in his chair, dead. One of the cops goes up to him with a pad of paper and says, "What's your name, sir, and what's your problem? . . . You'll have to speak a little louder, sir." Maybe you had to be there, but it took the edge and the depression off of it. In fact, we had to laugh.

When I started on the force, I had a captain tell me a lot of men didn't want women cops. He said he didn't either, but he'd help me be the best. One of the things he told me was to rely only on myself. He said I wouldn't get the backup that men would. He was right, too. When I was walking a beat and saw a fight in a bar, I would call for backup before I entered and broke up the fight. On the way in I'd see police cars pulling up with the cops sitting in them, just watching—just to see how I'd do, I guess, see if I'd come out.

Saving a captain's life was one of the highlights in my career. I was working during the Pan Am Games, and I was downstairs in the basement. Some cops asked me to come up and help the captain get his breath. I get up, and he's turning blue. I cleared his throat with a Heimlich, gave him CPR and mouth-to-mouth. I got him breathing and then called the paramedics. They said I'd saved his life.

Once, a partner and I carried a man out of a burning building.

I'm sorry to retire. I want to see more black cops on the police force. I still don't want to see black people abused. I guess I am still thinking of those cops in Mississippi who ran us in for swimming in our motel's pool.

Chris Saffron
(retired)

New York Police Department

Chris Saffron worked undercover narcotics in West Harlem. Recently retired, he owns and runs his own security, investigations, and intelligence firm.

I worked undercover narcotics for the NYPD, mostly in West Harlem in New York City. I'm in my thirties and was a cop for twelve years. I joined the force for all the usual altruistic reasons. I wanted to help people, and I couldn't see myself sitting in an office. I needed an outlet for my energy. The NYPD seemed like a home for me.

The job was hairy. I've been assaulted more times than I can count. One of the things that scares me the most, however, is heights. Drug arrests often require setting up OPs (observation posts) on top of buildings and outdoor fire escapes, and I'm afraid of heights. Often I'd freeze on the fire escape on the way up, saying to myself, What are you doing here? But I felt so good when I made the arrest, I guess it made it all okay.

Often when I get to the top of the building and see the buy go down, I have to tear back down the fire escape, arrest the dealer, and lock the guy up. Racing down an outdoor fire escape, for me, is hairier than making the arrest. Every inch of the way I'd have to stop myself from freezing in terror.

I had two incidents undercover that really got to me. The one that scared me the most involved a shooting—my first shooting incident. It was in West Harlem near 112th Street. I'd already been there once to make a buy, arrested a dealer, but the other had gotten away. My bosses wanted me to go back to the same corner that same evening to look for that guy and see if I could find him and another guy as well. That's always bad. I've known a number of officers who have gotten killed that way—sent back to the same corner after a bust.

A former supervisor once told me that the CIA station chief in Beirut, William Buckley, got killed that way: When the American embassy in Beirut was overrun, Buckley's cover was blown, but the CIA director William Casey sent him back into Beirut anyway. He was captured within two weeks, tortured for several years, and killed.

So if you are an undercover arresting officer, you don't want to go back to the scene of an arrest the same day you made an arrest. It is very dangerous. People will remember you, and most of those people live there. You can end up like Bill Buckley.

But they sent me back in anyway.

A block away from the corner, I saw this huge guy under a scaffolding. He was wearing a red polyester shirt, bulging with prison gym muscles, and was sitting on a chair. I'm thinking, What's he doing at two thirty in the morning?

So I approach him. I'm looking scraggily—like a junkie. He stares at me and says, "What you want?"

"A fix."

He walks me toward an alley. I figure he's going to go in, get it, and bring it back, but he wants me to come down the alley. Oh shit, he's going to mug me and take my buy money, I'm thinking.

I figure he's so big, he isn't going to come at me with a gun or knife. He'll probably take a swing at me, and if I'm ready for it, I shouldn't get hurt too bad.

Also he's so big and flashy in his red shirt, if I call in, he won't be hard to find.

So he takes me down this alley. There's a gate at the end. He reaches up between the top of the gate and the housing for something, and I think, Shit, he's going to do me. He's getting me the drugs.

I take my eye off him for a split second to reach into my pocket for the buy money. When I look up, his right hand is swinging at me, and I can't see what's in it.

I know it's a bottle when it shatters against my head, and I go down.

Now I'm on my back, and he's lunging at me with a broken bottle. I pull my piece and fire. He also drops to the ground, and I think, Oh, God, I've shot him. But it's so dark and I'm so dizzy, I miss him.

Now, it didn't stress me at the time. I've been assaulted making buys countless times. But there was something about the fact that I had to shoot that bothered me. The truth is I'm a fighter, not a shooter. I could tell you innumerable stories where I've been justified to shoot. There was one time a guy came at me with a machete, and I still figured out how to fight him. I always found a way to get around it. This was the first time I couldn't. I had to fire my gun. I was on my back and had to pull my piece.

Even now I get sick to my stomach when I think of going out for buys. It really affected me.

In fact, one of the reasons I wanted to get something smaller than my nineteen-round Glock 9-mm was that a smaller gun is less likely to kill somebody. A friend claims I'm more afraid of killing people than getting killed.

One time I thought I had killed somebody. I saw a guy selling ounces on the street from a hiding space. This time I couldn't hide atop a building. I was street level. Sometimes I'd hide in an alley, sometimes a doorway. This time I was just in some shadows. I mean nothing between me and the buy but shadows.

And this dealer has five lookouts—including his "wad man" (the man with the cash) and his "stash man" and his "hand-to-hand guys"—and I'm fifteen feet from him, hiding in a shadow. Just as he's handing off an ounce, I jump out of the shadows to collar him and recover the ounce.

Now, sometimes the lookouts will jump me—especially if I try grabbing three of them at once—but a lot of times they're too scared. I come out very aggressively, and also they aren't looking to go to jail. I mean, what do they get out of all this anyway? Not enough that's worth going to jail over. Especially if in the process they injure a cop and end up doing major time. Most of them just want to haul ass.

In this case, they all split. I chase the seller into Fort Tryon Park, tackle him, roll him onto his back, and he starts punching me. So I hit him with my Maglite and he relaxes. But still he'd thrown the ounce into the woods. I cuff him while he's unconscious, call the emergency service unit for a pickup, and go looking for the ounce.

Finally, I find it, but when I come back, I hear paramedics saying, "Is he going to make it?"

Meaning, is he going to die?

Then I see the perp and there's a crater in his head. I can see his brain. I realize, Oh no, I did it when I hit him with my Maglite.

I can see it all now: an inquiry board, internal affairs, the whole nine yards.

It turns out, however, the perp was a stand-up guy. He actually exonerated me. He said he shouldn't have hit the officer and that the whole thing was his fault. I hit him in self-defense.

I should mention that this guy was a Washington Heights Dominicano. The Dominican drug gangs up there are like that. For drug dealers, they are astute businesspeople—clean, intelligent, they don't rat each other out, and they don't do drugs. They have a code. If they fight you and lose the fight, they understand that. They also want happy customers and repeat business. They always say, "Come back here. I'll be nice to you. I'll take care of you." They're always fair and honest in their dealings.

The dealers in West Harlem frequently try to roll me for my buy money. In fact, I once got jumped by five guys up in Harlem with clubs and guns and got banged up pretty good. Still, it didn't affect me as much as when I shot at that guy near 112th Street.

Once, when I was in uniform, my partner and I got a call to apprehend a dangerous cat. We get to the apartment, and the two men there say the cat is wild and has bitten one of the guys. They assure us that the cat has never left the apartment and doesn't have rabies.

Well, the guy rolls up his sleeve and the arm is mangled. It needs at least sixty stitches. I'm wondering if it's a cougar.

They assure me it's a house cat, but now my partner's getting scared. I'm saying, "Hey, it's just a cat. I'm not about to call a SWAT team to take out a cat."

So I get their biggest wool blanket and a laundry hamper. My partner is to pepper-mace the cat, I'm to throw the blanket on it, then drop it in the hamper. But we can't find the cat.

Finally, we're in the middle of the room, and I hear a howl straight out of *Alien*.

The cat attacks my feet, rips up a new pair of Timberland boots, moving so fast it's like a Tasmanian devil, not a cat. I've never seen anything move so fast. I turn to my partner to say why didn't you mace it . . . and he's gone.

He's hiding in the kitchen behind a closed door, but I get him back in the living room. Now the cat is climbing straight up the wall like a spider. My partner maces it, and it drops to the floor. Both our eyes are tearing from the pepper spray and the ninety-degree summer heat. Still, I scoop the cat into the blanket and stuff the whole mess into the hamper.

Unfortunately, all I stuff in is the blanket. The cat's escaped and is now on me, ripping up my chest and shirt.

Finally, I grab him, get him into the hamper, and we haul him down to the ASPCA. All the while, my partner is bitching about how we should have called in a SWAT team.

Captain Sam Welch

Indiana State Corrections

Anyone who thinks that a corrections officer (CO) is not a law enforcement officer has clearly never been in a prison. Maximum-security COs, like Sam Welch, deal with more criminals in a year than most cops deal with in a lifetime.

Captain Welch not only prevents, stops, and breaks up criminal acts, he helps to rehabilitate offenders. He and his colleagues have helped to encourage many offenders to give up lives of crime.

Humorous, college educated, obviously fit, Sam Welch is a captain of corrections officers in one of Indiana's maximum security prisons. Sam was a Vietnam marine veteran as well, and he and his unit were often used as bait to draw in larger VC and North Vietnamese units. They were then to call in reinforcements—a military mission with much downward mobility. His military experiences probably prepared him for prison work.

Captain Welch has also witnessed many changes in the prison's culture in his three decades of prison work.

How'd I get into prison work? Ever since I was young, I liked helping people, and I've liked an active life. Let me give you an example. A close friend got a divorce, and the divorce wasn't amicable. According to the divorce settlement, she was supposed to get their SUV. Her husband wasn't eager to give it up. I'm sure he felt the settlement was unfair, and anyway he was now living in Gary, Indiana.

She came to my house and asked me if I'd drive to Gary with her to pick up the SUV. She'd talked to the Gary police. For whatever reason, they said they couldn't help her. They said, however, that if she had the papers, they'd let her take possession of it.

Now, her ex is a tough guy, and Gary is a war zone—often voted the most dangerous city in the United States. You sometimes hear it called "the Homicide Capital of the United States"—which statistically it often is. So I put on my Kevlar vest and got out some of my weapons, including a derringer, which I carry in my boot.

We basically know where he is. We're riding in that area, and we finally spot the SUV. He's in it, and we pull him over. He doesn't want to get out or give up the car, so I grab the wheel and send my friend to a pay phone to call the police.

Two cops come. They're white, in the middle of an exclusively black neighborhood, but cool. The ex, however, is not cool. He's glimpsed a pistol in my belt and starts yelling, "He's got a gun!"

A crowd gathers, and the cops look apprehensive. I tell them I'm a corrections officer and that I've got a licensed .357 on me. Breaking open the cylinder and shaking out the rounds, I hand them the gun and the bullets. They ask if I have any other guns. I tell them about the .38 derringer in my boot. They ask for it, and I break it open and give them that gun and bullets as well. Anything else? they ask. Actually, I had some knives and a ninja throwing star on me but decided to skip that.

I show them my driver's license, my gun licenses, my corrections ID, and my friend's divorce papers granting her possession of the SUV. I can see now it's a good idea I came strapped. Her ex is furious—so angry that the cops hand me back my guns and bullets, tell me to drive my car back where I came from, and tell my friend to drive the SUV back as well.

Her ex was so mad at them, they looked like they might lock him up.

I guess I always wanted an active life—even a little risk. When I got out of high school in 1968, I decided if I was going into the service, I'd go to Vietnam. After all, that's where the action was.

So I join the Marine Corps. Prior to joining the military, I'd never fired a weapon—not even a BB gun. I became a good shot, but when they tested us, they decided I'd also make a good communications specialist. I was upset. I wanted to get a gun and go into combat. I didn't want to carry a damn radio.

Well, the Vietnam War was on, and they needed men with guns more than radios. So they gave me my gun and sent me to war.

I was in a rifle company, and we lived pretty much in-country, which I kind of liked. You didn't have someone over you all the time. All we did was run ambushes on the other troops. We ran at platoon strength. In fact, part of our job was to act as bait—to draw in larger forces. We had squads out all day and all night trying to draw the enemy out, and when we made contact, we were supposed to call in firepower and the cavalry to finish them off.

Obviously, if you intentionally go into combat outmanned and outgunned, you run a very good chance of getting killed, and I saw a lot of my fellow grunts die. Those patrols were so dangerous, we used to tell ourselves we were already dead. That way we didn't have to worry about being killed. To some extent it was like that film *We Were Soldiers.* The strategy was the same. I must say, however, we weren't trained by colonels who then took us to 'Nam in a unit.

Most of the time when we saw colonels, they were in helicopters high overhead, complaining that we weren't chopping our way through dense foul mine- and sniper-infested jungle swamps fast enough.

It always looks easy from high overhead in a chopper.

I learned in Vietnam things weren't as I had imagined them. I saw what weapons and firepower could do to flesh. I learned that the Vietnamese were human beings who were fighting for their country and saw us as invaders. They were warriors just as we were.

I was small back then, barely 155 pounds—so small I even squeezed into a VC tunnel once. That experience scared me as much as I've ever been scared in my life. That tunnel was dark, narrow, went on forever, and I thought I'd never get out.

Before I went to Vietnam, I would have liked the idea of being a police officer. Not after 'Nam. 'Nam conditioned me to survive under extreme circumstances. I was afraid that if I was a cop—and I've had opportunities to join police forces—and someone pulled a gun on me, I'd shoot them. And I don't mean in the leg. I was trained to kill. Working as a corrections officer, you don't carry a gun. You don't even carry a nightstick. You have to use your brain instead of your sidearm. Still, prison work wasn't that different from 'Nam— at least in principle. When you first work behind the walls, the inmates are going to test you, see what you're made of, and maybe 'Nam did prepare me for that. One thing was for sure: After what I'd seen in 'Nam, those inmates weren't getting any cherry. They'd have to try real hard to rattle my cage. I've had offenders over the years tell me, "You're crazier than me."

So prison's not that much different from Vietnam—at least in principle. In Vietnam when you went out on patrol, you didn't know if you were coming back. You can walk into certain situations in prison, it's the same thing. You can't predict what will happen.

Let me give you an example, and this occurred after I made captain. One day I'm entering our industrial area—where the prisoners work on heavy machines, punching out license plates and stuff. We call the central area Main Street. I'm walking around a corner onto Main Street, and a melee breaks out. People are pushing, fighting, and I go, Oh shit. Here it comes. I see a couple of officers getting into it. They are way outnumbered, and I come up behind them to cover their backs and help out. Among other things, Main Street is filled with machines, tools, stuff with hard, sharp edges. It's the worst place in the world to have a brawl, but since fellow officers are in the middle of it, there's no way a CO can walk away.

Somehow, we all got out of that one okay.

Another time, I see this one big inmate—I mean really big and tough. Maybe six-foot-five, 350 pounds, a powerlifter who benches 600 pounds with reps, and, by the way, gay. He's coming out of the mess hall carrying two tomatoes. Now, we let inmates carry fruit out, but not vegetables. Of course, inmates have to test you, so when I tell him he has to throw the tomatoes in the garbage, he gets in my face. Seeing his attitude, another inmate eggs him on. Still gamin' me, he turns and walks away. I go after him and say, "Let me get your name and number."

He continues walking on. I walk with him, keep asking for his name and number, but he just says, "You better get away from me." It's his standard answer every time I ask for his name and number.

I've been trying to talk nice to him, saying, "Let's not make this any worse than it is. Let's talk about it."

He's not going peacefully, though, so I grab his arm and put him in a hammerlock. I grab his wrist and swing it up behind his back. It comes to an abrupt halt. His arm is going nowhere. He looks down on me like I'm an insect and says, "You ain't tryin' to break my arm, are you?"

Flinging me aside like a rag doll, he starts walking again. I get up, and I'm still walking with him. He's telling me to go away, so I get in front of him. He shouts at me to get away, clearly pissed, and pushes me, lifting me three feet off the ground.

Now a lieutenant's joined us, coming up from the inmate's rear.

The big man turns around to deal with the lieutenant. Luckily, I'd landed on my feet, so I jump on the inmate's back and get an arm around his throat. What I should have done—like they taught us in the Marine Corps—was to force a forearm around his throat, grab his elbow, and slip that arm's hand behind his head. Then it's fairly simple to choke him out.

Instead, I acted like a mama's boy. I got him down on the ground and tried to turn him around. The inmate was so huge, the lieutenant and I were like dogs trying to pin down a grizzly bear. He was throwing us off like we were nothing. Furthermore, he had friends gathering around him, shouting and screaming, urging him on. Violence in prison can break out like a firestorm at the smallest provocation, and the surrounding inmates looked ready to jump in.

A third officer joins us, and we're still struggling to restrain his arms, which is like trying to hold down a forklift. He's like Gulliver, throwing off Lilliputians, and I'm one of the Lilliputians. When we do flip him on his stomach and climb onto his back, he just does a push-up and bucks us off like a rodeo bull.

I try to get a fingerhold on him. I hear a finger snap, and I think, I got you *now*! Then I look down. It's *my* finger that's just broken.

We clamber onto his back after the push-up and the bull ride. He's still throwing us off, but then another officer shows up. The lieutenant's yelling, "Get his feet! Get his feet!"

Personally, I've given up all hope. Hog-tying this guy is like trussing up a tyrannosaur with darning twine.

The new guy is more optimistic. He's had no ring time with Moby Dick, so instead of giving up in despair, he hurls himself onto the behemoth's kicking legs, trying to lash his knees together with his . . . belt.

Loyalty gets the better of my fear. Instead of breaking for the gate, I also throw myself on one of those flailing feet, locking my own legs around his ankles, attempting to ride those legs down like an outlaw bronc.

He drives his thigh into my crotch like he's hammering a baseball out of Yankee Stadium. He drives my testicles straight into my stomach and halfway up my esophagus.

Another officer joins us, and we finally get his arms back—two COs on each arm—after which someone snaps the cuffs on him.

He still throws us off, however, like a bucking bronc, his face red as the tomatoes he tried to remove from the mess hall.

Ironically, I never lost my hat. My sunglasses, yes; my hat, no.

We eventually drag him to the bird hole—the shakedown area where we search people. The captain's office is also there. Staff takes him from us and shakes him down. We take him up to our lockup. I'm seriously pissed—something I let everybody in northern Indiana know. Among other things, I'd heard him tell the other officers we'd hurt him, and he wants to go to the hospital.

He's broken my finger into a hard right angle and blackened most of my right eye. My cojones feel like he's run them through a hammer mill, and he's blanketed my body with crimson bruises and purple contusions. As far as I can see he's pristine—pure as the day he vacated his mother, not even winded—but he's one who gets a free night in the hospital.

Why did I fear *I* would be reprimanded?

So we took him to the infirmary, and of course there was nothing wrong.

Still, he got his night in the hospital instead of the hole.

On the bright side, my finger only hurts when I'm awake, and my testicles only throb when I look at women.

One of the weirdest experiences happened when I was still a new corrections officer. We had a gang-affiliated inmate whom I had to escort to Gary on a funeral trip. The inmate had a bad reputation. He was doing hard time, and the Gary PD believed he'd killed a lot of people he'd never gotten busted for—in part, we believed, because he always killed rival criminals. We always assumed that the police don't knock themselves out investigating murdered crooks. Some of the cops I've known view intergang killings as a public service, a kind of psychopathic euthanasia. One cop I know calls the murder of murderers "evolution in action."

I was to take this alleged killer to a big public funeral, which was to be heavily attended by gang members and other criminals. We would be surrounded by mad-dog psychopaths—some of whom wanted him free, others who wanted him dead, all of whom wanted us in the ground. Furthermore, a corrections officer—except under highly unusual circumstances—isn't supposed to carry a firearm around inmates inside or outside the prison. Now, there were two COs accompanying the inmate, and the first officer did have a firearm. I didn't. So I was expected to both protect him from rival gangsters—all of whom we assumed to be heavily armed—and to stop him from escaping with friendly well-armed gangsters . . . while I was *unarmed.*

This is clearly an assignment with a lot of downward mobility.

Perhaps that's why someone dragooned me into this rapidly deteriorating assignment. I was young, new, and had no mentors to protect me. Someone had to eat the pipe, right?

I have no idea to this day how or why the other CO drew the blackball.

Maybe he'd pissed off . . . *God.*

I hasten to add I cannot imagine any supervisor today sending a young CO on a job like that. I can't imagine anyone sending an inmate into a criminal-infested civilian environment like that—not even surrounded by the entire 101st Airborne.

Just getting to Gary that day was scary.

We even had to worry about battling our offender's friends and enemies en route. We had to take a lot of back roads—remote country roads. Luckily, the inmate knew those back roads with a sickening intimacy and could redirect us when we got lost. Because—as he was at great pains to let us know—he'd dumped a lot of bodies himself on those back roads.

Not that the offender was happy about this route, either. He didn't think we were going to Gary at all. He was convinced someone had paid us to take him out—shoot his balls off and dump his body on these country roads. He was sweating and pissing blood the whole way. I was starting to sweat myself, and my bladder wasn't feeling too good, either. What *was* I doing here! Maybe the offender was right. Maybe my partner had been paid to kill him, and I was just along for backup. Maybe my partner was going to whack me, too. Who did I have to fuck to get out of this movie?

So we finally get to Gary. Some cops meet us, and we follow them to the funeral. It's in a church, and there's a crowd. As I walk up that church aisle, every criminal in Gary pins me with his sheep-killing eyes like I'm his own special . . . *bitch.* They all know we were headed there that morning. They've been waiting for us, gunning for us.

They know I'm . . . *unarmed!*

We're talking pimps in sunglasses, red ruffled shirts, wide-shouldered pink suits, and broad-brimmed hats. Hookers in skin-tight miniskirts with matching scoop-neck tops, strutting their ample stuff on five-inch stiletto spikes. Other prostitutes in short tight dresses with skimpy plunging necklines and big hats full of feathers—all of them with luridly crimson lipstick and fingernails—are flashing their voluminous wares and rolling their mascaraed eyes. When we stroll up the aisle, they leer at us as if we were johns about to whip out our bankrolls and then follow them into the parking lot for a little action.

Many of the men have ominous bulges under their armpits.

My partner's not exactly brimming with machismo, and Vietnam or no Vietnam, I'm so nervous I'm scratching my crotch and ass like they're on fire—never unaware of the fact that I'm . . . *unarmed.* I'm the one with a bull's-eyes strapped over my brains and balls. If someone wants to geld a guard and hold his castrated remains hostage—or just kill him outright—that guard is *me!* I'm the unarmed target of opportunity. I pose the least risk, maximum impact, the best of all possible returns on investment. . . . To the bad guys, I'm the weakest link.

And everyone in the church knows it!

We let the cuffed offender sit with his friends and family. My partner sits in the back row. I sit in front by the pulpit with one eye cocked over my shoulder to watch the guy and my other eye watching the front and sides of the church. When the service ends, my partner and I are on him like hawks. We grab his arms, and we all shoot straight up the aisle. People try to stop him to talk, but my partner and I are now beyond rude—achieving whole new dimensions of insubordination. This is no time to stand on manners.

On the way out we did U-turns, ran yellow, even red lights, barely missing babies in strollers, the elderly on walkers, Seeing Eye dogs leading blind people. We roared back to the prison, pedal to the metal, like the hounds of hell were at our backs.

Our heavily shackled friend in the backseat was even glad to get back to his cell. Nowadays we could never do that for an inmate. The people and the times are far too unpredictable.

Today, we face every kind of prison violence short of nuclear strikes. In fact, we do face nonnuclear bombs made from gasoline and paint thinner. We have to watch the gas in the lawn mowers, which our trusties use to mow the grass outside the wall and which we keep in the storage sheds. We have to watch the paint thinner. Inmates will steal flammable liquids a teacup at a time, store it up, then pass it on to friends or sell it to an inmate—someone who has a vendetta and wants to firebomb another inmate.

When I first started, the cells had multiple layers of oil-based paint. Sometimes someone would firebomb a cell, and the wall paint would ignite. The fire could become so intense that the heat would melt the bars. We couldn't even get a key in the lock to save the inmate. It'd melted. We'd stand outside his fire-filled cell and watch him burn and scream.

Which is exactly how the inmate I escorted to the Gary funeral was killed not too long after our trip.

We have dormitories here for some of the inmates. They live in three-sided cubicles, which we refer to as "cubes." The dorms house anywhere from 180 to 190 guys. They're allowed to get up and walk around pretty much the whole time they're in there. At night, if they ask permission, they can get up and go to the restrooms or the showers.

We had a fire in the dorms not too long ago. We had a very young inmate in the dorm, and someone doused him with a flammable substance and lit him up. He was racing through the dorm, a sheet of blue flame. Luckily, some people got a blanket on him and put it out. He was young, volatile, antagonized older inmates, and we couldn't protect him after that. We had to move him out of population. We may have to transfer him to another prison.

I would guess 60 percent of the inmates don't like the dorms. Our cells are all single occupancy, and the inmates would rather be locked in a cell where it's harder to get to them. We have had riots in the dorms, and we've had staff assaulted during these riots. When you think about it, 180 to 1 is not good odds. Hard objects are sometimes hurled at the guards and the inmates. Thrown hard enough, a large bar of soap can hurt you.

I know of one guard who got caught in the middle of a dorm during a power-out. Everything went coal-black, and inmates fired soap bars at his head like they were shot out of howitzers. If one of the inmates hadn't hid him under his bed, he might have been killed. Unfortunately, if you're a corrections officer and you want to do your job right and treat everyone the same, you can antagonize a lot of inmates. You write inmates up for infractions, and it might not seem like much to you, but it can cost them their parole later on. You cost them their parole, they'll *hate* you. Ironically, it's the honorable COs that may have to fear retaliation the most—the ones who try to treat everyone fairly and equally. When the lights go out, their enemies may look for revenge.

And it can get very dark and isolated in prisons.

One problem is that the inmates are there 24/7 and don't have much to think about. So if you anger an imate, you may go home to your wife and kids, but that inmate sits in his cell and broods. They also live in a culture where they have to settle their own scores and defend themselves from the other inmates. They can't call the fuzz. So the CO can't protect inmates 24/7, but he can hurt them occasionally. Many guards' write-ups are based out of necessity on imperfect information. If the inmate feels that a guard hurt them in an unfair way, they can find ways of getting back at him. After all, the inmates outnumber the guards many fold.

We worry a lot about gays in prison. They can get hurt and cause other inmates to get hurt. Our staff does random field checks looking for altered clothing—where gays alter the prison-issue khakis and white T-shirts to make them look more feminine—which isn't allowed. Sometimes inmates also try to wear their clothing in odd styles to convey gang affiliation. We have to watch for that, too, because a prison gang is infinitely more dangerous than a single inmate.

Do we do any good? We got guys that if they weren't locked up they'd be dead. We give them a chance to straighten up and find positive goals.

A lot of them do and lead decent lives.

I try not to learn what the inmates did to get into jail. One time we had a prisoner who I learned was a child molester. That knowledge so altered my attitude toward him, it made me unprofessional. After that, I didn't want to know what inmates had done. Only if they're a security risk will I look at their packet, their file jacket.

We let inmates keep cats in the cells if they get them registered. They keep them on leashes because they can get out between the bars.

Ironically, even though I'm black, I have more problems with black inmates than white inmates. Let me give you an example of one white racist inmate I had to deal with. One of the most dangerous, racist inmates we had was nicknamed Blue Eyes, or Blue for short, and he was death on blacks. Blue was so bad, he would only talk to a couple of corrections officers, period. I was one of them—despite his implacable, unrelenting hatred of blacks. I just let him know what the rules were and promised him I would never lie to him and never did.

Blue respected that. Honesty among guards is not universal. A lot of guards come from bad neighborhoods themselves, and some of them even identify with the inmates—at least initially. That can lead to inconsistent behavior. Sometimes guards will lie to inmates just to make their shift a little easier or to get through a difficult situation.

I don't deal that way with inmates.

Blue picked up on that and used to talk to me.

We have Aryan Brothers, KKK, all kinds of racist gang members in the population. The white racist is not eager to confront a black CO. He doesn't want a black corrections officer correcting him and giving him ultimatums in front of other white inmates. He doesn't want a black man humiliating him in front of his peers. On the other hand, if you treat the man fairly and respectfully and he knows he can't play you and you won't play him, he'll tend to take the path of least humiliation.

The white Klansman or Aryan Brother might treat a black CO better than a Blood or a Crip.

Black inmates, in fact, will sometimes see a black CO's fairness as being unfair to their shared racial identity—and to racial solidarity. Some black inmates will take me aside and say that since we're both black and suffered the same shit from "the Man," I'm supposed to let them bend and break the rules. When I don't, they say, "What you doin' this to your own people for?"

That I treat everyone the same and that I'm consistent—they can't understand. They don't understand that we might both be black, but *they* aren't law-abiding blacks, and *I'm* not an unlawful criminal.

They still think, however, I should treat them differently.

Some black inmates—when I don't give them special privileges—call me a "race traitor" and "the white man's nigger."

The white racist inmate, on the other hand, doesn't expect special treatment from a black officer. He's happy if a black CO doesn't publicly humiliate him.

A black CO, however, has cultural advantages over a white CO. A black officer is more likely to understand the cultural idiosyncrasies of black inmates. Some black inmates just have to act up and shout smack at the COs. They can act and look pretty intimidating in the course of this showboating. Some white COs don't understand they're just fronting and may get out the mace. A black CO may just wait them out, let them run down, then get out the cuffs and say, "Cuff up. Let's get this over with."

When I came back from 'Nam, I spent some time in college. I studied business and learned accounting. To this day I'm only six credits short of a degree.

When I first applied to the prison, in 1977, I had my applications in to other places and was offered an accounting job. I just couldn't see myself in a suit at a desk crunching numbers all day.

Like I said, I need to be active.

When I started out in '77 we had 5 percent black guards. Today it's 50 percent.

I feel you always have a choice. I tell that to inmates all the time.
I tell it to myself.
I have seen progress.
Who says there's no such thing as progress?

Chief James Butts

**Formerly of the
Santa Monica Police Department**

James Butts—former chief of police, Santa Monica Police Department—is tall, handsome, witty, and urbane. He is highly sensitive—genuinely moved when he looks back on some of his experiences—and in very good physical condition. He looks to me like he bench-presses Buicks. Chief Butts has had some very dramatic experiences.

I was a college basketball player at Cal State, intent on going to law school. After a knee injury and operation, however, I needed part-time employment to pay for both my new car and school. I got a civilian job with the local police, and when the application test came up, some of the cops encouraged me to take it. I got one of the higher scores and was offered positions in a number of departments. I went to Inglewood, planning to stay a year or two—until I paid off my car and saved some money for law school.

Around Christmas 1976—after my second year—I was assigned to robbery detail, working tactical alarms. These alarms had a box in the back with an antenna that signaled us when the alarms were tripped. Most nights, we were responsible for four locations.

One night, as soon as we settled into our unmarked car, we got a call. The robbery was two blocks away. We were there in seconds and spotted them taking off in their getaway car. I floored it, and we were in high-speed pursuit.

Since our vehicle was undercover, it didn't have its own radio. We had to use our portable, so no one knew where we were. We could see these little flashes coming out of the Dodge Challenger we were chasing, sort of like fireflies, and heard this weird *tinkle-link tinkle-link.* At first it didn't register what was happening. Then we heard a crash, and one of headlights went out.

"Shit, man," I said to my partner, "they're shooting at us."

It was the first—but not the last—time I would be shot at.

My partner had had maybe three years on the force, I'd had two, and this was not what we'd expected. We were now slinking down on the seat. We heard more *tinkle-link tinkle-link.* We saw more flashes, more flashes, and then the radiator was hit. *Tinkle-link tinkle-link.* "I'm busy driving," I said to my partner. "You got the shotgun. I suggest you get busy."

Every time the car made a turn and we were parallel to it, my partner fired at it. Finally he hit the windshield, and they spun out. We both jumped out of the car, yelling, "Freeze! Freeze!"

Still they were moving around in the car, firing occasionally, and wouldn't come out. We were now in radio range, however, and could reach fellow officers on our portable radios.

We waited for backup. It seemed to take forever—though it was probably less than a minute and a half. Finally we heard sirens, saw lights, and police were coming from all four directions— Glendale, Sheriff's Department, the LAPD. Word had gone out that cops were alone, taking fire, and in pursuit. Sixty or seventy officers showed up.

We arrested them. One was on parole for robbery, the other burglary, and they'd decided to hold court in the street. One got nine years, the other eleven.

I know there's a lot of rough stuff in police work. Racism exists, but I also knew at that moment when the chips were down, we were a band of brothers and sisters. I still get choked up thinking about it.

When I was working metro, some guys robbed a bank only two blocks from the Inglewood police station. My unit supervisor approached that bank while the robbery was in progress. It was "a takedown robbery." Two guys with semiautomatic carbines had everyone on the floor.

Now, my supervisor's undercover, and while he's got a pistol, it's nothing compared to what these guys had. When he sees the guys through the glass, he puts it out on the radio that there's a 211 in progress. He gives the location, description, and everyone's coming. The guys, however, are also coming out of the bank. He engages them but is outgunned. They make it to their car and take off. They hit the main drag, dead center in the middle of the city, and ten police cars minimum are on them. One of the robbers, however, blows out his back window so he has a panoramic view and opens fire. It's like a shooting gallery. He's blazing away with semiautomatic weapons, and we can't shoot through our windshields. He's picking us off one by one, blowing out windshields, cars crashing into trees. I mean, two guys retired after this chase. One of them was a motorcycle cop who got shot in the chest. His vest saved his life, but he ended up with heart trouble.

My partner and I were third in line. Then the first two are shot out of the pursuit, and this is the second time I've been shot at. The first time I'd heard *tinkle-tinkle,* but now I'm getting shot at with supersonic rounds. I'm hearing, "KA-BOOM! KA-BOOM!"

Now, this is scary as hell, and finally one of the rounds goes through our windshield, making a small hole in it but disintegrating the rear window. My partner is screaming, "I'm hit! I'm hit!"

It turns out he's got glass in his eye.

We continue after them. The chase winds around into Los Angeles, and finally the suspects crash into a palm tree. By now their escape vehicle has taken a lot of rounds. The irony is that the two guys aren't riddled. The driver is hit once in the head—and dies. His partner is also hit once—a graze—and ends up doing a lot of time for robbery and murder.

I've worked SWAT teams, metro, robbery, narcotics. If I counted them all up, I've probably had seventy or eighty truly dangerous experiences. I've been shot at five times and seen guns out thirty or thirty-five.

SWAT was obviously dangerous. Robbery was amazingly dangerous as well, because we worked those alarms. When you answered a tripped alarm, a robbery was often in progress. People ask why I do it. That's easy. I love it. If I didn't, I wouldn't be any good at it. In my early years, I used to come in on my days off because I was afraid something would go down, and I wouldn't be there for it.

Some of the things are hard on you and will kill you if you don't learn to compartmentalize, if you internalize them continually. When you see people gagged with duct tape, their hands bound, lying in bathtubs, shot in the back of the head, and you think of their last moments of terror and there was nothing they could do, it tears you apart. Things involving children you can't escape. Too much of that will screw you up.

The biggest difference over the years is that police departments are now externally driven, more responsive to the culture around them. Attitudes have changed, and departments which couldn't change have suffered.

Cops have changed. They're no longer from the military. Today's young cops grow up on TV, video games instead. On the other hand, they are better educated, more questioning of authority, more inwardly driven and focused. Cops in the old days were part of the prevailing culture, not necessarily that of the community they policed, and would sometimes participate in things they probably knew were wrong. But they had the sense that no one knew cops but cops, that it was us against them, that police departments were a world unto themselves, and they were far less questioning of what is right and what is wrong.

Cops today have to be more understanding of the world around them. They can't stand apart.

After six years in Inglewood I was promoted to sergeant, two and a half years later to lieutenant, two and a half years after that to captain. At that point I was able to have an effect on police policy and knew I'd made the right choice.

Eventually I became the deputy chief, and in 1991 I came over here to be the chief in Santa Monica.

Detective Lester N (retired)

Michigan City, Indiana, Police

Lester Norvell—a former college basketball player with a degree in marketing—is still athletically fit. He spent well over thirty years in law enforcement, a fair amount of that time undercover.

I was a marketing/sales major in college but was unsure what I wanted to do after I graduated. When I returned to northern Indiana, I had friends on the police department. They encouraged me to go into law enforcement. I'd always been active and had gone through college on a basketball scholarship. My college roommate—whom I played basketball with—was on the force and eventually became the chief of police. I guess I liked the idea of having an active job. I ultimately worked in almost every division—plainclothes, everything.

The funniest thing that happened to me didn't seem funny at the time. It was a rainy day, and we received a call that there was a heart-attack victim being delivered from Joe Phillips Airport to Saint Anthony Hospital. We met the car on Michigan Boulevard and escorted the victim to the hospital. We were going ninety miles per hour up the street. The rain was coming down in torrents, and I lost control of the car. All I could do was skid. I skidded right into a car lot and stopped three inches from a new Chrysler. Everyone laughed like hell, though I didn't.

The scariest things I did were when I worked undercover in narcotics. I was used as an operative in surrounding cities. You never really know who or what you might run into. You have little, sometimes no backup. Still, you're going to shady places to meet shady people. I was there to buy anything they had. I went to Gary a lot, and it is statistically "the Homicide Capital of the United States."

A lot of towns around here can be rough. We have a big maximum-security prison in one of them, and a lot of men, when they get out, stick around and operate their scams out. A lot of times they line up local women while in prison and move in with them when they get out.

I've been in a lot of big cities, known a lot of big-city men and women, and I've come to conclude that any trouble you can find in Chicago, L.A., New York, you could find in some of those small northern Indiana towns.

Working undercover, you have to be strong-willed. The sellers will try to get you to use drugs or get you drunk. They ask you a thousand questions, trying to shake you. They want to know why you want them, why you won't take the drugs in front of them. I'd just say, "Hey, man, I ain't here for a job interview. I'm here to buy drugs."

Funny thing is, they're so greedy, as soon as they see that money, all their skepticism goes away. It brainwashes them. I've had men say, "Man, I know you're the police. I don't care. Just give me that money." As soon as they see the money, it's a done deal. That's why they go to jail. It's always dangerous. You talk about taking someone's freedom from them, you don't know what they're going to do. You're out there alone with little or no backup. You can still get burned.

You have to have some actor in you to work undercover. You have to wear a lot of hats. Because the criminals don't know you, they always suspect you're a policeman, and they're always pushing you, looking for some confirmation or refutation. The big thing though is to never let them know you're afraid of them. Let 'em know you're just as tough as they are. You don't create a confrontation, but you don't back down from one.

One of the most exciting things about working narcotics was the drug raids. I liked to kick in the doors. I liked to go in early in the morning when they were still in bed—hung over, drug-sick, tired, half asleep—and catch them by surprise. Who expects someone to kick in their door at five A.M.? You get surprise on your side. Catch them before they piss, we used to say.

Lots of time it was a team effort, kicking in the doors. We'd have state cops and cops from the nearby cities. It was all planned.

There does come a time when you burn out on undercover. You lose interest, you start asking yourself why you're doing this. When that happens—and eventually it does to everyone—it's time to get out. If you burn out, you stop giving it 110 percent of your attention, you make mistakes, and you get hurt. That finally happened to me. My concentration started to flag. I got out of undercover, and I worked it a long time. I worked plainclothes fifteen out of my twenty years on the police force. I did a lot of that time in investigations, but I did my share of undercover.

Back in 1972, when I first came on the police department, marijuana was a big deal. No one cares about that now. Cops are battling crack, heroin, meth, cocaine. Also back then, we knew all the players. There was a time I could walk the streets and knew everyone in town. Nowadays we have an influx of criminals from Gary and Chicago who come here to do their business. We bust someone now if they have Chicago drugs on them. That's the problem. The police don't know who the players are. Every day the players change, but the game stays the same.

The dealers are getting younger, and the older dealers turn to young kids to deal for them, because the young kids—when they're caught—don't do as much time. It's all about survival.

Then there are the gangs now. You live in a bad neighborhood, it's like being in prison. You have to belong to a gang to survive. You have to be affiliated to something. You can't make it alone.

I had one chase I'll never forget. It was nighttime, snowing hard, and five guys snatched a woman's purse. I ran a little in college, played basketball, so I jumped out the cruiser, picked out one of them—you can't get them all—and took off. I chased him through streets, alleys, over fences. I chased him forever. Eventually I caught him. He waved something at me, and it looked like a gun. I put my piece on him and shouted drop it and hit the ground. He did, and it was drugs, not a gun.

I cuffed him, took him to the courthouse, and it turned out he'd escaped from prison in Pennsylvania and was wanted all over the country. He'd committed a number of violent crimes. Why I picked him out of the five, I don't know.

I've had a lot of car chases. When I was young, I'd go after almost anyone. Later, I'd try to get close enough to get the license plate, and let my radio do the rest. If someone's killed someone, that's a different story. All cops will go after them. You chase him all the way.

One of the most satisfying things I did was once when I was driving up Lake Shore Drive. I saw some people crowded around a woman on the ground. My partner got out of our cruiser, and I cleared the people out. I did CPR, and I had an ambulance bag in the back of the car. You place the air bag over the mouth and force some air into them. I kept her alive, and when the paramedics arrived, they said she'd have died if I hadn't taken care of her.

She wrote a big letter thanking us.

Now I work in work release. I've gone from locking people up to helping them adjust to society and become a productive citizen. Right from the start I tell the men I don't think they're a bad person. I tell them, "You did something bad, but that doesn't mean you're bad." You try to give them a sense of value.

Hemingway talked about a lost generation. This is the lost generation—the generation of babies having babies. They walk around with no hope, no ambition, and they often turn to drugs. The grandmothers raise the kids because the mother doesn't want to miss her youth. She wants to have fun and party.

It takes a village to raise a child. When I grew up in the projects, if a woman saw you doing something wrong, she'd beat your behind, then call your mother. When you got home, you got some more motivation from your mom. Don't think of saying, "I didn't do it." Your mama would say, "You callin' Mrs. Jones a liar?" Then you'd get a double whuppin'. Nowadays, you put your hands on a child, you're in trouble. That even goes for the parents, too. Children around here challenge their parents to hit them. They threaten to call the authorities on them. "I'll call the DCFS, Mom."

Work release can be satisfying—especially when you see someone's attitude change and you see them go on to do what you told them to do and make something of themselves. You know then you made a difference.

Before that, I did federal work release. I was a caseworker for people coming out of federal lockups. I'd counsel them and find them work.

One problem I had both then and now was getting guys out of prison who want jobs but are high on drugs. How can you get a job when you have drugs in your system?

Nowadays, you tell kids the way things used to be, and they don't believe it. It sounds too wonderful.

Kenny Brown

**Beverly Hills Police Department
Formerly of the Philadelphia
Police Department**

My first experience in enforcing the law was the law of the Monroe Doctrine. I was part of the barricading of Cuba during the Missile Crisis. I was at Guantánamo Bay, in the navy, when the Russian navy steamed into the Caribbean—apparently loaded with missiles and nuclear warheads—and I was on one of the U.S. ships that turned them back. It was hairy in that our ship was just out of dry dock, where we'd been undergoing repairs. We had no fire power, no planes, no torpedoes, no nothing. We hadn't even had time to load on ammunition for our big guns. When we swung our guns around on the Russian fleet, ours were empty.

One lesson I learned from that was never take an empty gun to a gunfight. That's a rule I've lived by as a cop.

I studied hard in the navy. When I took the police exam, I scored high marks, and I could choose the area of police work I wanted. I lived in Philadelphia, loved horses, loved watching the Philadelphia horse police, and so I chose horse patrol.

I guess I became a police officer because I wanted to ride horses.

Those horses were wonderful. You could ride them anywhere—into the center of downtown traffic, into the airports, into rainstorms, snowstorms, crowds. They were great animals—well trained and thoroughly disciplined.

My most exciting arrest on horseback was when my partner and I were called to a murder scene. We galloped to it and found the victim sitting on a sidewalk with his back against a building. He was slashed from throat to chest to waist and was sitting in a pool of blood. He'd been killed for his boom box.

A woman on the third floor leaned out the window and pointed to the killer riding down the street a block away on a bicycle with the boom box blaring.

We galloped up the street after the bicyclist-murderer. Without any planning or warning, we caught up with him. There, in mid-traffic, we hooked his arms with ours and lifted him off his bicycle seat, blaring boom box and all, while the riderless bicycle continued on up the street. It didn't fall over till we had the cuffs on him.

One of the scariest episodes again occurred on horseback. An officer had been attacked by a gang. My partner and I got the call, and we took off on horseback. The officer was surrounded by about thirty gang members and was crawling under a car for protection, while they stomped him. When they saw us on horseback, they scattered. I chased one of the gang leaders, who'd been kicking him up an alley. As I was gaining on him, he turned and pulled a gun. Now, horses don't stop on a dime, and I'm reining him in, screaming, "Whoa!" and staring into the gun barrel.

Luckily, my partner was coming up the alley from the other side and ran him down. But I still remember charging into that gun barrel: It just kept getting bigger and bigger and bigger, and I had no place to hide.

You remember some terribly tragic events, too. One time I was on patrol, and I came across a traffic accident. A car had been rear-ended. There were young children in the car, and the doors were jammed and wouldn't open. As I got out of my car, the gas tank, which was in back, exploded. The whole vehicle was on fire. The heat was so intense it was scorching the paint on our car. We couldn't get close enough to help them. All we could do is stand and watch.

One of the funnier calls I got was from an old woman who wanted me to drop her off downtown. She thought I was a cabdriver. I tried to convince her I wasn't, but she wasn't buying. I finally gave up and drove her downtown, at which point she began arguing with me about the fare. I told her I could not accept any money. She still wouldn't listen, and kept shouting, "I'm not going to pay you more than five dollars. I'm not going to pay you more than five dollars."

When I started out, there were fewer guns and less drugs and more respect for cops. It's changed completely since then. Now we have to carry mace, extra guns, extra magazines, extra cuffs, rubber gloves. When I started, none of this was necessary. People had respect for police officers.

Of course, it's also true that when I started out, you really had to mess up to end up in court. Nowadays, people are dragged into court all the time—for divorces, drunk driving, harassment cases, nuisance suits, civil suits. They are more prone to see the people in blue as the enemy. Things have changed an awful lot in the thirty years I've been a police officer.

Commissioner John O. Boone (retired)

Massachusetts State Corrections

Police are not the only law enforcement officers. Some corrections officers deal with more hardcore criminals in one day than many cops will see in a lifetime. They are charged with deterring crime and catching criminals in the act of crime just as surely as any cop on the street, and inside the prison walls they have countless criminals committing crimes. Part of law enforcement is also preventing crimes, which includes convincing criminals that the criminal life is a bad place to be. That is an important part of their job—and ours.

One of our pioneers in corrections work is John O. Boone. His distinguished career goes back fifty years. He has worked every job there is in corrections—from prison guard all the way up to state commissioner of corrrections. In fact, John Boone was the first black commissioner of corrections in Massachusetts.

I went to college by way of the GI Bill. I majored in sociology and economics and received a master's at Atlanta University, specializing in psychiatric social work with delinquents. During a practicum at the New York Training School for Boys in Warwick, I worked with Claude Brown, who would later write *Manchild in the Promised Land*. When I got my master's, I was offered two jobs: one with the Veterans Administration and the other with the Atlanta Federal Prison.

I opted for the federal prison system and went on to hold every job from guard to parole officer to caseworker to group psychotherapist to caseworker supervisor to chief of classification and parole department to superintendent of the Lorton Correctional Complex outside of Washington, D.C., to Commissioner of Corrections of the Commonwealth of Massachusetts.

I'm often asked why I was drawn to prison work. I believe my interest in prisons began in childhood. My father used to take me with him to visit his cousin who was on a Georgia chain gang for illegal possession of a firearm.

The chain gang was in a wooded catchment area, guarded by two white shotgun guards. None of the prisoners were balled and chained on visiting day, as they were on the public roads during the week. It was a carnivallike atmosphere with hordes of black male inmates, families, and friends, like a Saturday-night fish fry, but everybody was welcome to partake in the corn pone and the black-eyed peas and salt pork boiling in the big black pots.

Vice and contraband abounded, bartered by the trustees, who shared their loot with the prison officials. Conjugal visits, married and unmarried—sometimes involving prostitution, which down through the years had been exposed by the Atlanta newspapers—were available for a price.

My father also took me to hear Governor Herman Talmadge speak in city hall, where the jail was located, about the cost of maintaining prisoners in Georgia. I remember him saying, "No nigger is worth more than fifty cents a day, and no white man's worth more than a dollar."

My father and I were among the handful of blacks who dared to come to that speech. I believe my interest in prison and prison reform began in those days, when I was just a toddler.

By the way, I also received another lesson back then concerning crime and punishment. My father's cousin, who was locked up for that firearm, was only in a short while, but when he was released he started keeping that same pistol under his bedroom pillow. My sister—believing it to be a cap pistol—shot my younger sister in the shoulder and herself in the knee. I know it sounds strange, locking a man up for possessing a firearm—particularly in the Georgia of that time, when so many people owned guns—but part of me also recognized that if he hadn't had the gun, my sisters wouldn't have been shot.

I'm often asked what was the most exciting or dangerous thing that happened to me in all those years behind prison walls. That one's easy: the Lorton Prison Riots of 1968.

Lorton was 90 percent black, and throughout the 1960s, prisoners' rights activity had been boiling across the country, fueled in part by the Civil Rights Movement, the Vietnam War protests, and the various student protests, as well as the bitterness and frustration of being behind bars. Campaigns in many prisons for a Prisoners' Bill of Rights were under way, and bloody confrontations in many prisons were a possibility.

Several things led to the riot—complaints about visiting privileges, sanitation, food, the treatment of inmates in solitary, and in particular the guards' aggressive attempts to crack down on those they labeled "troublemakers." However, two "acts of God" also foreshadowed the riots. The first involved lawsuits by prisoners over the repression of their religious beliefs and practices. The litigants included both Black Muslims and white prisoners. The second "act of God" was an electrical storm which blacked out the prison.

The prison went up in flames, and the inmates ran riot.

I was superintendent of Lorton and had tried to establish a rapport with the prisoners. I understood their grievances, had always had an open door, and tried to work closely with both them and my staff.

I took an active roll in quelling the blacked-out blazing anarchy which was now the prison. I went down into that fiery inferno that was the yard and met with them personally. They were afraid of reprisals and so I went without armed protection. Many had hidden themselves throughout the prison, frightened both of inmates and the eventual return of the guards.

I explained that I wanted all the inmates in the big yard. I didn't want inmates or guards cornering prisoners later on in dark hallways and injuring them. I felt if everyone was out in the open, we could secure them more efficiently—and with less brutality. Also it would be a positive sign to the guards—who had to deal with them day in, day out—that the inmates were cooperating. I thought that might improve relations.

Also, the local fire unit would not enter the prison and put out the fire unless I could guarantee that all the prisoners were secured. They did not want inmates jumping them from out of nowhere while they fought the fires.

I eventually got most of the prisoners out in the yard. There were still five hundred left. Luckily, some of the prisoners remembered that some of the inmates were still locked up in "the hole." I thought they'd been freed. Now they were in danger of being burned alive.

We got them out safely.

The guards were growing impatient. Many were in favor of a sweep—ferreting the prisoners out of their hiding places and punishing any of the so-called troublemakers, whether they were hiding or not.

Part of my negotiating posture with the inmates was that it was just me and them—no armed guards. We were negotiating in good faith and seeking a nonviolent solution. I was working desperately to keep Lorton from turning into a bloodbath.

Just as I thought we were about to achieve that, I saw six prison guards enter the yard through the side gate festooned with riot gear and gas masks. Tear-gas canisters bombarded us from the walls.

The prisoners felt deceived, and I retreated under a hail of inmate bricks. I was struck and still carry the scars. Had I been hit in the head, I would have been killed. To escape the rain of bricks, I dived under buildings and hid behind pillars. I finally made it through the side gate through which the riot team had entered.

The inmates went back into hiding, and now many of the guards really wanted a sweep. Still I argued against it. I got a bullhorn and bellowed into it for the inmates to enter the yard, come into the light. I promised them they would be safe.

In truth, they were sad, sick, scared, and did not want a fight. When they began walking into the yard and the light, I felt like cheering.

We secured them back in dormitories with minimum bloodshed. The injured prisoners we sent to the hospital.

Nonetheless, there was a sweep, during which inmates felt betrayed, unfairly treated, and brutalized. Guards wanted to return

Lorton to the status quo, while inmates were even more adamant about a Prisoners' Bill of Rights. It was a standoff.

I worked hard with both guards and inmates. I improved guidelines and management of everything from visitation rights to sanitation, to food, to expedition of money orders, and to the supervision of solitary confinement. I wasn't always popular with either side, but I believe when I left, I left Lorton better than when I found it.

For prison reform to work, both staff and inmates have to work together. I strove to achieve that.

After Lorton I went on to become the Commissioner of Corrections for the Commonwealth of Massachusetts, and thirty years later I am still working for prison reform.

Not a day of my life goes by, however, when I don't think of those visits with my father to that Georgia chain gang to see his cousin who had violated Georgia's gun laws. And I never stop thinking of my two sisters who were shot by his gun.

Robbie Robinso

Los Angeles Probation Officer

I was born in Washington, D.C., in 1953.

Out of wedlock.

When I was six days old, I was placed in a black foster home. It was a fine home. My foster father was an older gentleman who had served in the Spanish-American War. He would tell me stories of Theodore Roosevelt and San Juan Hill. When I was six, he passed away and was buried at Arlington with full honors. I still remember the funeral ceremony. The army chaplain spoke movingly of duty, honor, and country. The words resonated in me. To me they were more than words in a book. I knew then and there they were words to live by.

My foster mother, Mary Robinson, was an avid reader. Our home was filled with books. She read aloud to me every day and encouraged me to read. I was a good student, and even in grade school I read. I especially loved books on the American and Italian civil wars. In grade school, the teachers frequently asked me to stand before the class and tell them about the books I was reading. I would tell my classmates about the great Civil War leaders—including the Southern generals, Robert E. Lee and Thomas "Stonewall" Jackson, and Italy's great liberator, Garibaldi.

My foster mother was no holy roller, but she was religious. We were close to the church minister, and he would pick us up and take us back home every Sunday when we went to church. Neither of them smoked, drank, or used profanity.

Neither do I.

My caseworker considered my foster mother too old to be raising children. She was born in 1905, so by the time I was twelve, she was sixty. The social workers continually advised me to leave, but I refused. Mary didn't want me to, either. She even made several attempts to adopt me, which, among other things, would have cost her the state financial assistance she received for raising me. I also wanted to be adopted but the social workers wouldn't have it.

Nonetheless, we stuck together. I stayed with her until I was eighteen—longer than any of her other foster children—and went off to college.

I had to deal with a fair amount of bullying in school. Though I'm now over six feet, in school I was small, wore eyeglasses, and was a foster kid. The other boys would bait me, and I had to learn to fight.

In junior high school the physical harassment turned serious. The kids no longer fought one on one but attacked you four or five at a time. A small gang of these kids would approach you. The setup was always the same. The ringleader would say he wanted to talk to you. While he held your attention, the other kids would circle around you, then pop you in the back of the head. They called it "copping a Sunday." After I'd gotten gang stomped a few times, a friend told me how to handle these guys. As soon as the leader spoke to me, I was to hit him. I had fast hands and could get in four or five hard punches before I was knocked down. The gang leaders learned quickly that it wasn't worth messing with me.

Then in the eighth grade—when I began to take boxing and karate lessons—they left me alone.

In those days, Washington, D.C. had an excellent school system. My schools were entirely black, and the teachers instilled a great sense of black pride in us. Unlike today, where the kids are often taught to see themselves as victims, as somehow inferior, we were instilled with confidence. Those were tumultuous times. I remember when Malcolm X was killed in 1965 and soon afterward read his extraordinary autobiography.

I also remember Martin Luther King's March on Washington, and I remember both his and the two Kennedy assassinations. I viewed Bobby the same way I viewed King and was upset by both killings.

I had heroes. My karate instructors had all served overseas in the military—some in Vietnam—and were heroes, even surrogate fathers. They believed in staying strong both physically and mentally. They didn't smoke, drink, swear, and stayed married to the same woman. They saw karate as a thing of the spirit and gave me books—which I read—on its spirit and philosophy, including *Bushido—Way of the Warrior* and *Bushido: The Soul of Japan*. They didn't just teach and talk, either. They walked the walk. They still fought.

I would attend their tournaments and watch them fight some really rough guys—including Chuck Norris. They would tell me before the matches that the important thing was not whether you won or lost. No one wins all the time. The important thing was that you stand up to your opponent and that when he hit you, you hit him back. I would then watch them go out onto the mat and do what they said. Putting talk into action seemed to me to be crucially important.

They called that sort of courage "grace under pressure."

I was also very taken by the black actor Woody Strode. I loved him in *Spartacus* but was most impressed by him in *Sergeant Rutledge*. At one point in the movie, when he was getting hassled, he turned to his tormentor and said, "I ain't no dog. I ain't no swamp-runnin' nigger. I'm a man."

I loved the line, loved his attitude, and tried to emulate him.

Another man I emulated was our church minister, who still drove my foster mother and me to church each Sunday. He spoke to me with understanding, wisdom—never with condescension. He would talk to me about the world, about life. Quoting Proverbs, he would sometimes tell me, " 'Wait on the Lord: be of good courage, and he shall strengthen thine heart; wait, I say, on the Lord.' "

Memories of my foster father's Arlington funeral still haunted me. The words *duty, honor, country* still rang in my ears. My karate teachers had all served in the army, and street friends from the neighborhood were now returning from Vietnam. The military seemed to me a natural career choice.

However, around this time, a black teacher, Ms. Corley, suggested another possibility—college. Despite their military careers, my karate instructors confirmed her opinion, as did my minister, so I decided to give it a try. Ms. Corley helped me study for the SATs and recommended me to college recruiters.

It was people such as these who taught me the meaning of duty and self-worth, gave me hope for the future, even a sense of destiny—things which are sadly lacking today. Kids these days may have more materially, but mentally and spiritually are terribly impoverished.

I scored high on the SATs and went to Livingston College, an all-black school in North Carolina. My foster mother accompanied me on the train. We talked the entire time, and it was the closest I'd ever felt to her. I could feel I was entering a new phase of my life.

I was too small for football, and they had no baseball team, so I started Livingston's first karate program. I recruited a dozen kids for the team and set up tournaments around the state. There are pictures of me in the yearbooks surrounded by our trophies—though most of those were eventually traded to a local businessman in exchange for team-traveling expenses.

I worked hard and during those years beat more than a few state champs in tournaments. I was the only black karate star in the state at that time, and people respected me for that.

A history professor—a Dr. Halfond—encouraged me to go to

graduate school, and I went to the University of Southern Illinois, where I earned a master's in education. I graduated in 1980 and moved to Utah, where I worked as a counselor in their Upward Bound program. I worked with Navaho and Hopi Native Americans, encouraging them to go to college. I learned to ride horses with them in Monument Valley, and they called me Genee, which in Navajo means black. I sat in on their tribal meetings and was treated as a member of the tribe, something I have always been proud of.

In August 1980 I moved to Los Angeles. I worked as a trainer at the Holiday Health Spa, as a teacher's aide, and I taught in the city's recreation department and at a local Boys' Club. There, I met a black woman probation officer from the Crenshaw area, who had come to talk with me about kids who needed to do community service.

She told me I should consider a career as a probation officer.

She recommended me to the department. I filled out an application, went to interviews, and I started.

I began in Central Juvenile Hall. The gang problems were really starting to escalate around this time, and juvie hall was an eye-opener for me. I'd known D.C. gangs, had grown up surrounded by gangbangers, but the ones I got to know in juvie hall had attained a whole new level of criminality. These gangs commanded a loyalty from their members which was absolute, surpassing even family loyalty. They were recruiting ten- and eleven-year-old children, too—and training them to be soldiers, drug dealers, stone killers. In many ways, these child-soldiers were the most dangerous and terrifying gangbangers of all.

I also got to know some of the officers working in the Gang Unit—the probation officers who worked the L.A. streets and specialized in the gangs. I admired their pride, the way they carried themselves, and their esprit de corps. I knew someday that was what I wanted to do.

In the meantime, I worked juvenile hall and juvenile camp. I learned everything I could about the gangs in preparation for my eventual career on the streets in the Gang Unit. I learned the various signs, the gang language, the different levels of gang involvement, the various cliques and factions within the gangs, their differing attitudes toward music and the different rap-music rivalries. I learned their culture, their attitudes toward entrepreneurship and family.

Many times, this knowledge of their culture prevented violent encounters. In the cafeteria, for instance, there was always the potential for intergang violence. This was no small deal because there would just be myself and another officer surrounded by sixty very tough kids, and when fights broke out, hatred and mass violence could erupt with shocking ferocity. Furthermore, officers were unarmed and not allowed to strike the inmates even when struck. Breaking up a violent gang fight was no easy task.

The first time a fight broke out, the officer explained to me what had happened. He explained the mannerisms, the verbal exchanges— some of which were little more than grunts—the way they looked at one another. A more-experienced officer would have recognized that this was leading up to violence. He wasn't in a position to do anything, but I was. Had I recognized the signs, I could have prevented the fight.

I studied their world with a passion. I talked with them. I was especially interested in who their idols were. I can tell you they weren't Sergeant Rutledge, and they weren't mom and pop. What they told me about their mentors and role models would fry my hair. They introduced me to a whole new culture—a world I never dreamed existed. They became my teachers. They taught me. I also learned to detect differences. It's tempting to lump all people into a single bag, but in fact even in the gangs, people are still individuals. Not everyone is OG—"original" or "old gangster"—and hardcore. Some kids could be reached, could be saved.

In order to reach these kids, however, I had to learn what they expected of me. Did they want kindness, understanding, warmth? Did they only respect toughness, discipline, the back of the hand?

What I came to understand was they had their own code, their own conception of honor. In some ways, I had the same code.

I came to believe the virtue they admired above everything else was consistency, and I tried to behave that way toward them.

Camp was a great learning experience for me, and also afforded me a chance to help these kids. In camp there is lots of opportunity to talk with them, to develop case plans aimed at changing their lives around. During rec period I could take them aside, ask them what they wanted to do when they got out of camp. Did they want to go back to their families? To the old 'hood? What could I do to help them straighten up their lives?

Law enforcement is supposed to be about intervention, prevention, and suppression; and I've always been a big believer in police suppression. I've gone out on thousands of night rides with police officers helping out in the suppression of gang crimes, but in the camps I also discovered that gang crime is a kid issue. They're kids. I learned that in the camps. I saw them there—black, Hispanic, and white. I learned their problems—drug addiction, anger management, abuse histories, beatings, ignorance, and crime-infested environments. I had kids cry in my arms, and I heard it all.

And I think I learned how to get through to them.

"Yo, little brother, come here. Let me rap to you. I know you got some problems with the 'hood, your friends. Moms ain't the greatest, and Dad ain't nowhere. But you got to deal with you—with the issue at hand. We'll get to the other stuff later. And I promise you we will get to it. But right now we got to deal with you, with the issue at hand. Whatcha gonna do?"

I know in the camp I made a difference. I helped kids straighten up their hand. To this day, I run into a lot of those kids—grown men now—that I worked with twenty years ago, and they tell me about it. I hear about it all the time.

I have to emphasize—and this is very important—I am not and never was the only person out there looking after kids. There is an

amazing amount of help out there for them. There were lots of officers in juvenile hall, in the camps, and on the streets. And we all did
our bit. If they just opened up to us, we did them a lot of good. There
were special programs, with dedicated probation officers, teachers,
and counselors—who are out there trying to help them, even to the
point of putting their lives on the line—so I wasn't working alone. If
we could only reach the kids, we could put them into all kinds of
counseling and educational programs, including mentoring programs and graduate-equivalency-diploma programs.

Soon I began writing a lot of this down—what was happening,
what I was doing, what I thought ought to be done to change things,
and when my supervisors read what I wrote, they said I ought to be
in the field.

Which was where I'd wanted to be all along.

My first partner was Mel Heath, and he taught me a lot. He was
like an older brother to me and we worked West L.A., Culver City,
Santa Monica, and Venice. We worked with a lot of gangs—
Shoreline Crips, Santa Monica's 13th Street and 17th Street gangs.
Mel and I went out a lot at night, because that's when the gangs were
most active, and we wanted to catch them in their natural habitat.

When Mel left to become a supervisor, it hurt me a lot to lose
him. From time to time I still call him for advice.

When I started out, one of the things that struck me most power-
fully was how strong the gangs' power bases were. They commanded
unswerving loyalty from their troops, and their capacity for violence
and intimidation—particularly intimidation of witnesses—was terrifying. The best way to attack a gang is to get at its leaders, but that
wasn't easy. The kids, including the nine-, ten- and eleven-year-olds,
were fearless, and those who did collaborate were shot down like
dogs.

Furthermore, many of the gangs I dealt with were Chicano, and
in those circles you dealt with something far more menacing than
a single gang. The Chicano street gangs followed the directives

and guidelines of a group of prison leaders, known generally as the Mexican Mafia. This leadership is so powerful, it levies taxes on its members, which they extort from those in their neighborhoods.

For several years they were so powerful that they were able to declare open season on black gangs and collect their taxes from their neighborhoods, too.

When Edward James Olmos depicted some of this in his movie *American Me,* the Mexican Mafia murdered one of his technical advisers as well as a number of other people believed to have been associated with the film.

Nor is it safe working with the gangs as a probation officer. You are a much graver threat to them than a street cop. You put a person who's on probation behind bars basically on your say-so. You can enter their homes without a search warrant.

Sometimes, in fact, you enter their homes and referee family-gang disputes of frightening intensity. You are out there hassling drug dealers, rapists, killers, and psychos. You get caught in the middle of major-league gang wars.

All without a gun.

I've had assassination threats. My name has been blazoned on ghetto and barrio walls in big bright letters, letting the world know that there is a gangland price on my head and my days on this earth are numbered. Scaring them off is not an easy task, either. You're dealing with kids who are incapable of fear, who see murder and theft, dealing and intimidation as honorable trades, who view going to prison as a rite of passage, the road to becoming a man, whose jail and gang tattoos tell the story of their lives, monstrous memoirs terrifying to behold; whose rap-music industry—which so often glamorizes their crimes—is sometimes run by gang leaders.

I've arrested killers, gotten indictments against all odds, found witnesses brave enough to withstand intimidation, gotten cases to the point that justice can be done.

Then seen overworked, overwhelmed judges cut the killers loose out of misplaced sympathy or dubious technicalities.

And I've seen my star witnesses killed.

Over the years, I've seen the gang culture evolve. Twenty years ago, gangbanging consisted largely of dressing in gang attire and being down with your set. Fifteen years ago, gangsta rap entered the gang culture as a kind of gangsta bible and also in some cases injected money into the gangs.

Today, the gang culture is characterized by a complete disregard for human life and a near-pathological obsession with making money.

In working with the kids, it is nonetheless important to see them as individuals. Sometimes you get a kid who has potential, wants to do the right thing, but is being pulled down by his neighborhood. I had one kid I can think of who was a good student, a football player, but who was getting nailed for smoking dope, getting porn off the 'Net, and hassling teachers. Instead of sending him to a long-term disciplinary camp, I put him in a juvie hall for fifteen days. Afterward, I did extensive follow-up, which is critical.

In another case, I worked with a young man who was doing poorly in school, beating up his girlfriend, and bringing bangers home, terrifying his mother.

I recommended six months in a work or military camp.

Needless to say, most kids are resistant to probation officers. Street kids are notorious for not reporting to their probation officers. They bolt, climb out third-story windows, and jump. They will even fight you. Sometimes you need cops to help you converge on the kids. Sometimes when you visit the gangs, they erupt into fights and you have to break up their fights. Or sometimes it's between rival gangs you're breaking up.

Sometimes you have to surveil the kids from observation points from which you can videotape kids doing everything from selling drugs to assaulting people, including buyers. It's astonishing that you can videotape these kids committing crimes and they'll still deny it even when you have them on tape.

I've had to learn the differences between the gangs of conflicting cultures and between our gangs and those of different cities.

Chicago has a completely different gang structure, which we called "the Chicago Style." Different L.A. gangs attempted to penetrate Chicago gangland, but they met instant unified resistance and were almost immediately run off or killed. The Chicago gangs were amazingly cohesive and well organized to the point of running people for political office and mounting intense lobbying efforts on behalf of gang-friendly legislation.

The black L.A. street gangs tended to be entrepreneurial, money driven, fragmented, and fratricidal. They were for being "down for the 'hood," the 'hood being everything. They were desperate for "licks and kicks." A classic lick was a bank job (though some made vast sums in the rap music business), and kicks were mostly getting high through sex and drugs.

In the Latin gangs, everything was "*mi familia,*" all the various gang families reporting back to their leaders in prison. On the L.A. streets, the Mexican gangs pretty much controlled the drugs, and the rivalry between the Mexicans and blacks was intense. In camp, the two groups seldom talked; in prison, never.

The hatreds ran so deep, they had to be celled apart in prison.

The black gangs tended to be different from the Hispanic in critical ways. Where the Mexican gangs reverenced the older brothers, the blacks looked down on them. The second-generation gang members are much more reckless and violent. They see no consequences for their actions and see their older OGs as weak sisters.

Monster Kody Scott—coauthor of the bestseller *Monster: The Autobiography of an L.A. Gang Member* and whom, as a probation officer, I had dealings with—typified some of the L.A. gang extremists.

He describes in the book—and his brother, Little Monster, has described on TV—their gang activities, including the vicious gang wars, the drive-by shootings, murders, torture, years in jail, and their hatred of American society.

Monster has now adopted an African name.

The intense Monster-style destructiveness of these gang wars is a story fraught with many personal tragedies. One death that haunts me to this day occurred in the Valley. A man in the community who owned apartment buildings, worked with the city-council people and community leaders to get junkies off the streets, raised money for the community, provided jobs, and made it a better place was shot to death on the street by gang members. He'd personally brought reports of gang activities to the city council, and we knew it was a gangland slaying because he had a pistol of his own and killed two gang members before he died.

Afterward, his killers went down the street to a lawn party to celebrate.

I knew who was responsible and with the police built a case against his killers and arrested them. The case was overturned on a technicality, and they left laughing from the courthouse. I seriously considered leaving the force, but after taking three days off, I pulled myself together, swore to be a better probation officer, and promised myself that one day I would see his killers behind bars.

One of them has gone away for selling narcotics.

After that, I worked even harder. I studied the backgrounds of my kids before making my recommendations. I've helped send a lot of kids away for stiff sentences—frequently to get them out of a hopelessly gang-infested environment. I've also given lots of kids a second chance, after finding out that they did have positive things going on in their current lives. In those cases, I've done extensive follow-up. I would not just send them back and let them do the same old stuff. I've had witnesses who have stood up in the face of gang threats, testified in court, and helped me and the police put kids away—who had thought they were untouchable—for long terms. If those witnesses can stand up like that—I've often thought—I can, too.

The life of a street-gang probation officer is never dull. Most police officers will tell you how they fear most of all domestic calls, where they walk into an apartment—especially in a ghetto or the barrio—suspecting that their might be trouble within. You may walk into love and kisses or you may walk into SKS armor-piercing bullets.

I have seen kids jump out of two- and three-story windows upon my entrance into their home.

The life has gotten me into lots of major motion pictures—including *L.A. Confidential, Lethal Weapon* 1 and 2, *Starship Troopers, Courage Under Fire,* and *Marked for Death,* in which I typically portray the criminal element which I've spent the last twenty years trying to put behind bars. I'm told I play these roles authentically and authoritatively. I should. I've spent a lot of years living and working in that environment.

I've also done a lot of stunt work, and I sometimes think that all the time I've spent jumping out of apartment windows after fleeing offenders has prepared me for that.

I also get a lot of speaking gigs. I'm asked to talk on everything from street crime to gang life to the crack culture. I would like to say I'm an expert on these things, but no more so than many, many fine police officers and probation officers and corrections officers all over this country who are working with young people and trying to make a difference.

I would have to say that L.A. probation officers are probably the most respected in the country. Through the camp system—which, to the best of my knowledge, is unique in its extensiveness—and the involvement of POs [parole officers], we are able to save over 40 percent of our troubled young people.

Still, there have been nights I've come home and cried, talked to my wife about finding another job, and pleaded with God for things to change.

The gang culture in L.A. is so insanely self-destructive that I'm not sure sometimes if I will ever understand it, but one thing I know:

Until we do understand it, we will never change it.

I also know this is what I was born to do and will be an L.A. street PO as long as the city is willing to have me.

Captain James Carneygee

Corrections Officer

Captain James Carneygee has been a corrections officer at a maximum security prison since 1985. James has a quick wit and a philosophical bent, which no doubt helps him on his job. In one year, his job puts him in contact with more criminals than most policemen see in a lifetime.

Twenty years ago when I started working in this prison, old-time correctional officers—mostly retired—tell me that prison work was radically different when they started out in the 1950s and '60s. Back then—before corrections officers faced the sorts of gang and drug problems that are routine today—the prisoners were more organized, less fragmented, and enforced a lot of their own justice. For instance, if an inmate wanted to kill another inmate, the prisoners had a secret board to forbid or to authorize it. The inmates had a good reason for controlling the inmate violence.

Whenever there was a killing, the guards—in the course of their investigations—would lock the inmates down and were also capable of physical violence. Rumors persist to this day that inmate punishment could be coercive—very coercive—especially if the officers thought an inmate had information pertaining to the killing. So the inmate board determined whether the inmate had a serious reason for the killing to occur and whether it was important enough to suffer the guards' retaliation. The board was pretty effective, because if you went around them and killed someone, the board might well have you killed. If you committed a minor act of disobedience, the board might not kill you, but they would have someone beat the hell out of you. At least, that's what we were told.

One thing is certain: Prisons back then were safer and more orderly. Now—with all the gangs and drugs—it's a different world and culture.

At least, that's the way the old-time COs used to tell it.

Today, we have a different kind of inmate, many of whom are gang affiliated. We also keep some of the inmates in dorms, which we didn't do when those old-time COs ran the prison. To stay in a dorm, the inmates once were supposed to be thirty years old, but now we have teenagers in the prison dorms—that's how crowded prisons are.

We have nowhere else to put them.

The teenagers feel threatened, and their insecurity can make them dangerous. Older inmates are more mature. They've seen people live and die. They're looking to do their time and hopefully get out. The young kids, though, have seen so much death on the streets, seen so many drive-bys, so many drug killings, they aren't afraid of death and they don't care about killing. They don't even care about dying. If they feel threatened, they have no inhibitions about lashing out.

Positive feelings? What's a good day in the prison? If, at the end of the shift, nothing bad happened, we all go home feeling good, like we did our job. Believe it or not, many, many of these inmates will get out and lead productive lives. If we can keep the predators from stabbing and robbing and raping those who want to become positive citizens, we've helped everyone here. If no one escaped, if no one got hurt, we feel fulfilled. We helped to save someone. At least, we gave some of them a better chance.

Once I had an offender who couldn't read or write. His illiteracy so humiliated him he tried to hide it. I told him to never feel humiliated around me. He could never let *me* down—only *himself*. I encouraged him to take courses. He not only learned to read and write, he eventually got out of prison and became a tutor and a teacher himself. In prison he found a mission. He still writes me. You can't help but feel good.

Once I was overseeing the recreation yard. A lot of inmates jog, pump iron, work out, practice martial arts. I noticed two inmates wrestling. I didn't think much of it, but then I saw them trading punches. I walked over to break it up. Suddenly, violence spread through the yard like a virus. All the inmates on the yard started fighting. Inmates poured out of the gym . . . fighting. Luckily, no one attacked me, and I kept the two fighters that inspired the brouhaha on the ground while I waited for backup. The instant reaction of the inmates shows the kind of tension inmates live under and how quickly they can explode.

We have a lot of gang activity. Gangster Disciples, Aryan Brothers, KKK, Mexican Mafia, Bloods, Crips. They're there, but they try to stay inconspicuous. Whatever you have on the street, we have them. Every so often you see them throwing gang signs and sporting gang paraphernalia. A gang's potential for death and destruction is far, far greater than an individual's. To the extent that we break up and disperse gangs, we divide and conquer. It's the only way you can run a prison.

Inmates assault COs with unfortunate frequency. If you work the cell houses in maximum security long enough, you will be assaulted. It's inevitable. For one thing, inmates don't want you to catch them with drugs or weapons. So if you're searching them and they're dirty with that stuff, they'll sometimes attack you. An assault beef carries less time in solitary and less time added to their sentence than getting caught with drugs and a shank. Inmates have assaulted me for precisely that reason. They figure they can stall my search long enough, divert me long enough with an attack, so that they can get rid of their drugs or weapons.

I have to work with the young COs. They sometimes look down on offenders and let them know it. I tell them we're all men and try to treat them accordingly. You treat them like men, they'll treat us like men. At least, that's my hope. If you trash-talk them, on the other hand, they'll get back at *all of us*. Pretty soon we're all having trouble. If you set out to deliberately humiliate inmates, you hurt all the corrections officers.

In the old days, COs tended to come out of the military. Today, they come out of the civilian population. Some of those COs come into prison looking to prove themselves the same way some people join the Special Forces to prove themselves. Some of them see this as a battlefield in which you must destroy the opposition at every turn. That is a lose-lose philosophy that hurts everyone around them.

We get a surprising number of inmate self-mutilators and inmates that habitually assault staff. They end up in cells with round-the-clock surveillance cameras. We also have an excellent psychiatric staff—something that was lacking when I started. It's important because we get a lot of disturbed people in prison—people with suicidal tendencies, for instance. We will actually segregate those prisoners and put suicide watches on them.

One of the odder problems we have is the prisoner that won't leave his cell—often to change cells or go to lockdown in segregation. Sometimes he's afraid of other inmates—sometimes he's just losing it mentally.

This can be both frustrating and dangerous. You never know how crazy and deadly he is—what weapons he may have concealed. We have to send a five-member extraction team in with specialized equipment—helmets, shields, padded shoulder gear, leg and elbow gear. If the inmate has a history of weapons, the point man has a stun shield. Each member has a role. One man puts on the leg shackles, another the wrist shackles, another handles immobilizing agents. We also videotape everything because the offender may sue. They may claim you didn't warn them, inform them, and that we assaulted them for no reason.

We had old-time inmates who were really tough. If they said, we aren't going to cuff up for an officer, they meant it, and if you needed them to cuff up, you had a fight on your hands. The young kids, they'll create a commotion, refuse to come out of their cells, but then they will come out quietly and cuff up. It's all bravado, making a fuss to impress their young friends, but then not backing it up.

Years ago, the tough guys didn't want a gang. But if you crossed them, they'd kill you. Today we have a lot of cutting but probably fewer per capita killings each year.

One of the weirdest killings I ever heard of in prison involved a lightbulb replacement. An inmate complained that his bulb had gone out. Inmates do that kind of maintenance, and when he left his cell, some inmates changed the bulb. When the inmate returned to his cell and turned on the bulb, it had an incendiary explosive inside. The bulb detonated and burned up *two* cells.

I like prison work. You get to keep bad people off the streets and give those willing to change a chance at redemption.

Lieutenant
Valinicia Renee Washington

New Orleans Sheriff's Department

I grew up in Marrero, Louisiana, a suburb on the West Bank of New Orleans. I was raised by two loving, hardworking grandparents. My grandfather was a seaman.

I had no aspirations to be a police officer in my earlier years—I wanted to become a doctor. But my plans for medical school were put on hold in my teens when I was faced with a baby girl to raise. Soon after that, I met, fell in love, and married.

For several years, I worked for South Central Bell, the local telephone company. I took a leave of absence for the year to be with my daughter before I went to school. During that time, one of my neighbors mentioned that the jail in Jefferson Parish was hiring. I applied and got a job there as a booking officer. The jail system had a rotation schedule for their employees, which gave everyone the chance to work every aspect of the job. It was required in order to get a raise. The work involved contact with criminals, searching female prisoners, and lots of paperwork.

But the only problem was that the female officers also had to guard or escort prisoners. And I thought that was too much harassment.

I was harassed constantly, as were the other female guards.

I was offended and insulted, but the prisoners were already in custody, and the most I could do was to write them up. In fact, they had more rights than me as an officer.

I started looking around for another position within the law enforcement system. Every other job position in the sheriff's office that wasn't a secretarial position or a dispatcher, you had to go to the academy.

I elected to enter the academy. I began working for the sheriff's office on November 24, 1977.

One of the first situations I handled was being called to a scene where three or four neighbors were fighting with lawn equipment. Everything from lawn-mower handles to ax handles. When I arrived on the scene, the perpetrators were really going at it. They were really trying to hurt each other. The whole neighborhood had come out of their houses to watch, and to defend the people who were trying to kill each other. We—the police—were very quickly viewed as the bad guys.

There were three officers there, and we placed ourselves in a triangular position. I was the mouthpiece. I tried to talk the neighbors out of hurting us. I told them that more officers would be there shortly, and if any of us were to get hurt out here at all, the whole street was going to be burned to the ground. "Every stone is going to be unturned, and none of you are going to get away with this," I remember saying.

It worked, because the fighters and the neighbors who were cheering them on backed down quickly.

When the troops did arrive, half of my department had come to the scene in anticipation of a miniriot. It had gotten so out of hand, and we were terribly outnumbered, there was nothing we could do except stay in a triangle shape and protect our backs. And I remember thinking when I got in the car, Whew, if I didn't have this mouth we would be dead.

I always did have a gift for saying the right thing at the right time. I had a guy one time put a gun to my head, and I talked him out of that. I told him that he had more to live for, and that this was a temporary situation. If he shot me, he knew he'd face the death penalty. Why make a final decision about a temporary situation?

I pointed out to him that he hadn't done anything real bad, but if he pulled that trigger, there would be no hope. I reminded him that he had a couple of kids. I told him, you know, who's going to raise your kids? Who's going to be there to explain to them why it's bad to take drugs and why it's not good to get involved in sex early and about AIDS. He just kept looking at me, and finally I said, "You know, both of us want the best—you want to go home to your family, and I want to go home to mine. Right now, it's just me and you in here, and nobody has to know you pulled the gun on me." I told him that I'd let him off if he took the gun away from my head. When he started crying, I knew I had him. Eventually, he gave me the gun and was arrested.

He was charged with trying to shoot an officer, despite my promise to say nothing. But I have no regrets about lying to the man. He could have been a threat to another officer who may not have known the perp had that in his character. The incident left me a little weak in the knees.

One of the more humorous incidents that happened while I was on patrol was when a call came in about neighbors fighting, and one of them was armed with a shotgun.

I happened to be around, just around the corner, when the call came out. So of course, I'm the first officer on the scene. And when I get there, there's just this large group of people in the street, and you really can't see what's going on in the middle, but you assume that's the fight.

Police officers are trained to never go into a situation like that alone. But of course, that was exactly what I had planned to do—to wait for backup. Except that several people ran to my car to tell me that there was a man bleeding to death. I was told that the attackers had beaten the victim with a shotgun.

So, contrary to my training, I got out of the car. I went over, and here's these two guys, one of them is bloody from head to toe and the other is standing there with a shotgun."

I drew my gun to get the suspect to the ground. When I was about to cuff him, his girlfriend attacked me from behind. The girlfriend jumped on my neck and I threw her off and faced her.

So now I have to deal with her, and we're fighting, and the suspect gets up and disappears into the crowd.

A few minutes later, the girlfriend and I are struggling, and of course I'm winning. The girlfriend is screaming and yelling, then the suspect comes back.

Out of my peripheral vision I see the green outfit he was wearing, and I see he's got a gun. I jumped up off his girlfriend and stood in front of the suspect. The girlfriend screamed at him to "shoot her, kill her, shoot her, kill her."

We were on a driveway that was right next to a grassy area where we were fighting, when he decides to pull the gun up. He wavered for a moment, lowering the gun, and I took the opportunity to dive between a truck and a car, fifteen or twenty feet away.

The suspect fired some shots. Sometime during the fight with the woman, I had dropped my own gun.

There were two vehicles in the driveway, a truck in the front and a car in the back. He proceeded to run up, and I took a position on the ground so I could see where he was. I saw him coming toward the truck, where I was, so I got up and moved my location to the other side of the truck.

It turned into a Three Stooges routine with the suspect and me running around and around the truck. One of the bystanders had picked up my gun and was trying to hand it to me the whole time I ran around the truck, but I kept missing it.

Eventually, I stopped and faced him, both of us out of breath. I told him, "If you're going to shoot me, you may as well go ahead and shoot me, because guess what? I'm tired. You look tired and out of breath. You know, there's no sense in us running around this stupid truck anymore. So, hey, if you're going to shoot, shoot. I'm just too tired to fight with you. But, remember, if you shoot me, they're going to kill you."

And I stood there, half dressed from the fight with the girlfriend, who had ripped the buttons off my uniform. The suspect eventually decided not to shoot me.

I was badly injured in the fight—I ended up with a broken rib and severe cuts on my hands. It was the only time I was really injured bad in a fight.

I later sued the suspect for trying to kill me while I was performing my lawful duty. I won in court, a first for a police officer.

But he wasn't a bad guy. He didn't have a criminal record. He just lost control that day and got into an argument with his neighbor, who threatened him. They struggled over the shotgun and he got the upper hand, then butt-stroked his neighbor with the shotgun.

The girlfriend was really bad news. But I got my satisfaction that day. She couldn't win the fight, that's why she wanted him to shoot me, I guess. And guess what happened to him? Two years later, he was killed in a bar by a woman. I think it's ironic that a woman killed the man who had tried to kill me.

It was while I was working for the sheriff's department that I found my niche—working cases involving sex offenses and rapes. The unit was called the Personal Violence Unit, and I was very good at what I did, primarily because someone had molested my own child, someone who had been close to me and my child.

I went into the unit after that. I think I was very successful with the cases because I had an advantage: I saw and lived all sides—the reactions of the child to what was happening, the parents' responses, the perpetrator's actions and behaviors. This was a unique perspective for the department, to have an officer who had been through an act of molestation with her child. It made the situation unique for me, and for many years, I was really gung ho. I don't think I could have afforded to let the emotions step in my way as much as my desire to prevent this from happening to another child. Or to make sure that if it did happen, the child was vindicated.

I developed very close relationships with most of the victims I helped. Over the years, I sent them Christmas cards and stayed in contact. In fact, I still have contact with many of them. They call me from time to time and tell me what they are doing in life now. Many of them have told me that it was just so important to know that a human being who really cared for them investigated their case.

Knowing that someone cared about them as an individual made the victims feel that they could trust more easily, and they could trust the system. I would take time to explain everything to their families and the victims. I let them know that they could contact me at any time if they had questions or fears or nightmares. I pretty much made myself available to the victims and their families all the time.

One of the most memorable cases for me was the three-year-old who had been molested by her uncle. It had been a case of generational molestation, in which the uncle had molested three generations. The victim in this case was a little slow and she couldn't explain her story. Despite not being able to articulate what happened to her, the child was able to illustrate with dolls what her uncle was doing to her. The perpetrator had harmed her so much that she would try to perform oral sex on everyone at school.

There was just no justice for that child. She couldn't explain her story, she couldn't explain what he was doing except in the most simple terms. She did not have the mentality to be questioned or anything, so it was like this guy got away with harming this child. She was unable to protect herself, and her family wouldn't stand up for her.

Other family members who had been molested refused to go to court and support the young child because they didn't think there was any reason to dredge all that up again. To me, this was a betrayal of the young girl. I found it very hard to deal with.

Another case involved a man and his wife. Both were professionals. We were convinced that the father shook his baby, resulting in severe problems, including becoming blind. The district attorney refused to prosecute the case because the father was someone respected in the community.

They said the case was impossible to prove because the child was being cared for by a sitter. They were trying to nail the sitter. And I proved through the medical exams that it was impossible, this particular weekend, for the sitter to have caused the damage because the child had not been in her care. The injuries were more than forty-eight hours old.

It was clear that the father was the one who was caring for the child. He hired an attorney for his wife and refused to let me interview her.

It's indicative of guilt, whenever you go to talk to parents of a child that has been injured, and they tell you, "We have to get a lawyer to talk to you." The average parent who's not guilty of anything just comes in, they're very helpful, they want the issue resolved.

There were other ways that the father showed his guilt. When he wrote down his statement, and the child's history, he cried the whole time. When he started to write about the hours that the incident happened, he referred to his baby as "the" baby rather than "my" baby. Before that, it was always "my" baby this—I got up with my baby, my baby was crying, I held my baby—and then when it got to the point where we felt the injury was caused, he started saying, "The baby started crying, the baby wouldn't stop crying." This was a clear indication of guilt, this Freudian slip.

The subconscious change of pronouns in a statement is very indicative of guilt. You can't run away from your conscience. Nope, and that's exactly what he would need to do to survive that without any lasting effects.

As time went on, I realized that the system, in many cases, was unable to prosecute the perpetrators, and with that I became very frustrated. Often the kids were so young, they weren't able to articulate what had happened to them, or they would be faced with one parent who abused and the other parent would be totally confused. The confused parent would end up trying to handle the problem alone, and would screw up the case. And after the frustration, I just got to the point where I felt that I had to get out. I no longer wanted to know about this happening with kids anymore.

I just felt that I needed to do something else. I just woke up one morning and said, "I can't do this anymore." I took my concerns about my emotional health to the commander of the detective bureau and he told me he had a program he was working on for community policing.

When I stepped down from my position on the Personal Violence Unit, I had put in eleven years in that department. That was three years ago.

Nowadays, I head up the S.T.A.R. Program for the Jefferson Parish Sheriff's Office. S.T.A.R. stands for Survey, Target, Arrest, and Rejuvenate. I was one of the officers to implement the community-policing program.

I and several other members of the department developed a lot of the preliminaries. We searched records; we found out and identified where our most troubled areas were in Jefferson Parish. We also found out the names of our most repetitive criminals. From there, we developed what's called code 6 to address the criminals.

Code 6 is a special group of assistant district attorneys who prosecute the cases with repeat offenders. The same attorneys who track the criminal also prosecute the ones who return again and again to the same system. It's more efficient, taking the offenders to trial when their case is familiar. The body of the community-policing program is that the members of S.T.A.R. identify the troubled areas, go in one at a time, and go door to door, talking to everyone who lives within that area. We find out what the perceived problems are, and then we target those problems.

Some of them are crime problems; some of them are personal problems, or social problems. We've linked ourselves to all of the agencies that help to run the government, to ensure that we have a partnership with them to help us with special things, such as social problems or social situations.

An officer is assigned to an area after the necessary arrests are made, and he or she works to help restore the community to a livable state. The officer from S.T.A.R. works in addition to the normal police that are there and the normal 911 service. His or her job is to become familiar with the residents, find out who are the bad guys, and to develop a relationship with the community. Then, if something happens, people will come forward and provide information to resolve violent acts. So they stay pretty busy.

The way it works in a community setting is that the police officer gets to know the people in the community and they know him. And it's more successful because that officer has more time to get involved in family situations, or situations involving kids—the kind of situations that demand more attention. The officer is able to see a situation or problem through to the end. If an old lady can't get to the grocery store, he drives her, and brings her back. It's a more old-fashioned type of policing.

The New Orleans Sheriff's Department S.T.A.R. Program has been given nationwide awards the last three years running for being one of the top community-policing divisions in the country. I see myself as a leader. I enjoy what I'm doing now and can see myself still in the community-policing program ten years from now. Then I retire.

Officer Tanya Junior

Chicago Police Department

I am the mother of two young children and the wife of a Chicago police officer. I grew up in the Princeton Park neighborhood of Chicago, where my neighbors were friendly professionals—teachers, police officers. As a child I dreamt of traveling the world as a stewardess or a writer and photojournalist. I hungered for new experiences and to meet new people. I envisioned myself as a mother, but not as a wife.

A lot has changed over the years. My old neighborhood is now governmentally funded, housing welfare recipients. My dreams of traveling the world were never realized. I have found myself both mother and wife. And yet, I have never been deprived of new experiences and interesting people. My life path led me not around the world, but to the Chicago Police Department.

It was a circuitous path, at best. I paid my own way through college, taking some semesters off in order to earn more money for my education. I changed my major several times, searching for what was right for me. At age twenty-four, I was in the middle of my third major, information systems, when I realized it was not something I was excited about. I was afraid I would be in college forever and I realized I could make more money going into the police department than if I waited and got a job in information systems.

I intended to use the police job as a stepping stone. I planned to stay for a maximum of six years. Instead, I've stayed for fifteen years.

I joined the force in 1983 and was apprehensive about the job at first because I had little experience with police officers. The ones I knew were the fathers of my girlfriends who were very nice and funny people.

When I first came on as a young twenty-four-year-old with a younger-looking face, a tactical lieutenant tried to persuade me to become a tactical officer. But at that time, a lot of officers working plainclothes were getting shot. Quite frankly, I did not want to be among them.

Early in my career, I did work for six weeks in a high school. Though the instructions given to the undercover officers were vague, we knew there was a teacher who was selling drugs and young-looking officers were needed to pose as students. I started in the high school in January. I carried a full schedule of classes and had to do homework. I couldn't drive and needed to take the bus to school. I attended the school for six weeks, and though my supervisors checked up on me periodically, they offered no details or other in-structions. I didn't even know which teacher was under suspicion.

I wasn't allowed to tell anyone about the assignment. Other offi-cers knew I wasn't at work, but didn't know what I was doing.

At the time, it was pretty good, because I didn't have any friends on the job. Instead, I was making friends at the high school. One boy at the school tried to befriend me because he thought I was from another town. He would come have lunch with me, and one day he said, "I know why you don't come talk to us very much." And I didn't say anything and he said, "You have a baby, don't you?" I wouldn't say anything. He invited me to a party and I told him I would try to come.

About a week later, I got a phone call in the school office. I was told to leave immediately, without collecting any of my things. The investigation was ending. I was never told what happened. Since then, I've always been in a squad car as a beat officer. My first year was spent in the Eighth District. Since then, I've been in the Second District, the same as my husband. In that time, I found that I have a special aptitude for dealing with the public.

I wasn't trained to treat people badly. There are a lot of people who treat others badly, talk to them any kind of way, don't have respect for them, like they're not people. I deal with bad situations every day, but I understand that people just make mistakes. There are some people who are just downright dirty people. But a lot of people become angry and they just make wrong choices. And that's how they end up in a bad situation.

I have a lot of rapport with people I meet on the streets. Most people I meet, even after I arrest them, they say, "Thank you, Officer."

I especially like having contact with teenagers who might be headed in the wrong direction. I've found that when they won't listen to another adult, they'll often listen to me. I like to be able to make a difference in people's lives. Sometimes I even succeed in helping out adults who are making bad decisions.

I guess I have an aptitude for police work, but I'm not passionate about my job. Still, I take my work very seriously. I want to do my job right and I don't want to have that negative image. Unlike many officers, I prefer to maintain friendships outside of the police department. Most of my friends I've known since grammar school. And I rarely take my job home with me, even to my police officer–husband. We don't agree on a lot of stuff, so we don't talk about it a lot. He talks about it with his friends, and I talk about it with my friends. But we don't talk about it together too often unless it's something like a serial rapist, something major.

One of many tragedies I have been involved in did concern a possible serial rapist. Early in my career, I got a call about a woman's body that was found in an abandoned building by a salvager. The woman had been raped and shot in the head several days earlier. The victim's purse and identification were still on her, and I discovered that the victim's name was also Tanya. Perhaps that connection triggered a series of recurring nightmares which began plaguing me a year after the discovery of the body. I had been on vacation when I had the dreams and when I returned to work, I confided in a fellow officer about my dreams.

"All last week," I told him, "I kept dreaming about the girl who was dragged into the building and raped and shot in the head. We were going past Forty-eighth and Michigan and I kept seeing her in a building. It wasn't the building she was killed in. She was trying to get me to come into another building with her."

The other officer looked at me incredulously and said, "Tanya, would you believe that the same incident happened last week?"

There followed several incidents where a guy was dragging prostitutes into buildings and killing them. I don't know if the rapist was ever found, or if he was the same one who had killed the first woman, who was not a prostitute, but it was the same MO.

With so many women entering the police force, I don't see many obvious signs that they are not welcome. Younger officers who have joined the force in the last ten or fifteen years are more accepting of female officers than those who have been on longer. Still, a lot of men on the force just don't think a woman can do the job. They may not say it to you, but when they get with their friends they say it. Most officers won't let their views be known in the presence of a female officer, so it's hard to know how they really feel.

There are exceptions, of course. When I first came on the job, there was one lieutenant who would say to me on several occasions, "What are you doin' here? You should be home havin' babies." Or, "Why are you here? Didn't you go to college?" And I'd say, "Yes, sir." And he'd reply, "Why aren't you in college? Why aren't you in another job?"

At the time, I would just laugh and let the negative remarks roll off. I'd only had a year on the job at the time, and I didn't think there was anything I could do about it. I was afraid of my supervisors and

I knew that speaking out then, when there were fewer women on the force, probably would have caused more problems than it would have solved.

Now, if they insult me, I insult them back. I'm not intimidated by them anymore.

Early in my career, I was partners with a male officer who wasn't very comfortable with having females on the job. But we were together for over a year. When I came on, I was young. My district had a lot of officers who were experienced and they worked with you and helped you out a lot. At that time, the department was concerned about you getting the proper training. Today, the police department simply wants a lot of officers on the street, so they're rushing new officers through training and putting them with people who aren't really qualified to train them properly. In my opinion, an officer with only two or three years of experience is not qualified to train new officers. You just can't get enough experience, even in a fast district like ours, in two or three years.

The problem is the high rate of turnover among officers. Often, the budget doesn't allow for sufficient payment of qualified officers. Officers who are training are also limited in their ability to take vacation days. Often they resign because of the inconvenience.

I have been lucky in having, for the most part, trustworthy and competent partners. There was only one instance in which I got out of the car when assigned with a partner I didn't trust. Other officers could trust me, too.

I remember being paired with another female officer. The men would talk about how women wouldn't fight. But my partner and I would defend ourselves—we would really fight. We didn't have a problem with the men who worked with us. They knew that we wouldn't stand there watching them get beat up. I wasn't a fighter as a child, but did have to defend myself against older brothers. Once I attended a Catholic school, and Xavier U in New Orleans, I never had a fight again. Until joining the police department, that is.

One time a man was wanted for battery to a police officer. When the man was apprehended, they got him in the lockup, but somehow he got out. I was there when the man escaped. He was bursting out the door and I knew something was wrong. A second later, there was an officer behind him. I just started running. I got on the radio and stayed on, talking to them while I was chasing him. At times like these, when your adrenaline is going, you don't think about being tired. You just think about what you have to do. After you stop, you realize, I could fall and drop here.

The man ran into a housing-project building, seventeen stories high, with ten apartments on each floor. I went into the building with two officers who worked the public-housing unit and had an idea of where he might have gone. They lost him on the third floor, but someone saw him from the street. The man was on the sixth floor. Apparently, the man knocked on a woman's apartment and she let him in. When the other officers and I arrived, we asked the woman if we could check her apartment.

That's when the fugitive jumped. He broke both legs, but survived.

While we were standing there, looking at him and yelling, he jumped out the window. And before the ambulance arrived, a friend of his tried to drag him away. Other people were trying to drag him away from us.

I had another, more frightening, experience in the housing projects off of Thirty-fifth and the Dan Ryan Expressway. There had been a lot of shooting going on for several days at the projects, when my partner and I were called there to take a battery report. There were a lot of police cars in the area, but no one was getting out of their cars. They were simply making sure they were being seen so the shooting wouldn't be so bad.

When my partner and I arrived for the battery report, the projects were quiet. But when it was time to leave, the shooting started up again. We called for backup so the presence of other officers would quiet the shooting. It worked for a little while, but when we got to the third floor, bullets started bouncing off the walls around us.

That's the one time I was really scared. Sometimes you get a really aware feeling, really cautious. That was the one time I was really, really afraid. And to top it off, we didn't get the bad guys.

Some calls, however, involve criminals who are not so dangerous. One night, my partner and I got a call about an elderly woman who said there was a man in her house. When we arrived at the house, we spoke to the woman about the man. We asked if he was still in the house, and she said that he was and he was trying to do things to her.

My partner and I got the immediate impression that something was not right. We asked where the man was, but the woman confessed that no one could really see him. The woman said he was coming through her radiators and getting into bed with her. She said she heard his voice through her cereal.

Fortunately, the woman had family living with her and my partner and I were able to leave her, confident that she was being cared for.

Despite the dangers and the risks, I made a commitment long ago to not let my job change me. I don't fool myself into thinking that I have more power than I do, simply because I'm a police officer. As a police officer, you don't have any power. You're just there as a public servant. I guess my no-nonsense approach to my job can be summed up best by my husband and the risks we take every day. There were a lot of times that I have gone on calls where my husband was afraid or concerned, but sometimes you can't help it. You have to go.

Officer Roger Tucker

Philadelphia Police Department

I was born in North Philadelphia. At the time I was growing up, it was a middle-class black community. My grandmother and grandfather were about the only black Republicans in the area and I grew up with a pretty moderate lifestyle.

My mother was a quiet and gentle person. She went through a lot of trauma and turmoil because of my father. She subsequently changed to a very opinionated person. She and I got along, I guess it would be, begrudgingly. Whatever she thought of, she spoke on it. I think it served her well. That was the household I grew up in.

Although we didn't get along a lot of the time, my mother and I had a begrudging respect for each other. We had personal differences, like she liked blue and I liked yellow. She would say you should like blue and I would say, "No, I don't." I admit that I tried to become the man of the house. I had four uncles, and I looked to them for role models, and my grandfather provided a good role model as well.

Despite all the turmoil in my young life, my household was very stable and very established. My mother had seven brothers and sisters. I looked to that family for a lot of stability. They were the primary reason that I didn't end up going the wrong way when I was growing up.

Another reason that I didn't go the wrong way as a kid is that my large family would bring us kids to New Jersey during the summer months. I spent my summer vacations among aunts and uncles and cousins in rural New Jersey. It probably kept me out of growing up in the gangs and some of the other associations with city life.

Despite this highly chaotic upbringing, I think I had a fairly normal childhood.

My father was an enigma. He was supposed to be an orphan, but my family and I always suspected that he entered the country illegally. I never knew where my dad came from, and it turned out that my father was a bigamist.

I think he married six or seven times. He never got divorced. I have a multitude of brothers and sisters. The strangest thing is that he always named his sons after him. There are a whole lot of Roger Tuckers from here who live in upstate Pennsylvania.

I know of one brother in Philadelphia. My father always started a family, then when he felt it was time to move on, he left. He was original. "I'm going out for a pack of cigarettes," and then he would disappear.

I saw my father sporadically. He would come back every five to ten years. The last time, I didn't see him for fifteen years. I managed to see him before he died in D.C. His girlfriend had called me up because I was the only one listed in the phone book.

Nobody really knew about anybody else. My sister and brother lived in West Philly and I lived in North Philly. I got a phone call one day because my then-unknown sister and brother saw my name in the phone book and they were curious. My brother actually called up and thought I was his father. We talked on the phone and then we met and kind of established that our father had a family in North Philly and a family in West Philly. Then he moved to Johnstown, Pennsylvania, and then he moved to New York. From New York he moved to Detroit and from Detroit, someplace south. He ended up in Washington, D.C., before he died.

When I graduated from high school, I went into the army during the Vietnam War. I've always been an adventurer. That's why I joined the army. I had visions of going airborne and possibly becoming part of Special Forces. Instead, when I got to basic training, I looked around and realized that these people could get me killed. I don't mind doing it at my own volition, but I don't want to be ordered to do it. I had the technical skills to get into Ordnance and that's where I stayed.

I had always been interested in guns. Primarily, I guess the real background with me and firearms started when my father left and I assumed the role of the head of the household. I wanted to protect my household. I was six years old at the time, and I thought that being the head of the household meant that I had to have a gun. Initially, my guns were toys, but those toys only fueled my fascination with real firearms.

I spent most of my military time in Europe. There were riots over there at the time. A lot of the things going on were very similar to what was going on in the States. When Martin Luther King was killed, they had very big riots in Europe around all the same areas that the GIs were stationed. There was a lot of black-and-white combat in Europe, also. I didn't miss out on too many events while I was there.

Later, I came back to the States and was stationed in Fort Dix, New Jersey.

After I was discharged from the military in 1969, I ended up in the police department by chance. I'd gotten in town early from Fort Dix and the Philadelphia Police Department was recruiting. I took the test just as a lark, because I didn't have anything to do. In fact, I didn't even finish it. I kind of scribbled over the rest of the blocks because it was one of the computer tests with blocks. I filled in the rest of the blocks real quick and I turned it in.

But they sent me a note a couple of months later that told me I'd passed the test. I went to the post office and was told I had Veteran's Preference. I put an application in and waited.

I had an application in with the post office, and I ended up taking a job with the police department because it was the next job available.

The first three years in the police force, I worked in a district that was in the northwest part of Philadelphia. I lived three blocks off of the patrol-sector border and would often take my patrol car home for lunch.

I was policing my own community, but I also considered my police work to be mercenary work because I was policing my community for the majority of society, for their best interest. Where to some degree I was doing things for my community, to the larger degree and where my pay primarily came from was the majority community.

To some extent, I believe that I was hired to keep black people in their place.

To balance the scales, though, there is a black police organization called The Guardians. I ended up doing a lot of work with them—the marches, boycotts. We finally ended up with a court injunction on hiring.

This means that Philadelphia—this was back in the eighties, just before I left the force—is still working under the court injunction which states that a full 50 percent of the police-academy classes have to be minorities. A lot of cities have something like this court injunction. The year that I graduated from the police academy, it was the summer of the riots and the Panthers. You might have heard of the Great Panther Raid in Philadelphia where they stripped the guys in the street. I came out in 1970 or '71. It was in August. My first job as a rookie cop was to go down into the neighborhood I grew up in and put up barricades to keep the people out and to keep them away from the Panthers' headquarters.

I was putting up the barricades, a rookie in awe of the whole situation, and there was a crowd milling around. From the back of the crowd, somebody says, "You're Roger." I couldn't see who it was.

The man asked me what I was doing over there. I have been trying to answer that question to myself for a long time.

The man who asked me that question eventually ended up working for the mayor. One of the things that I am very much in agreement with is that a person has to see inside the system to make some changes, but the people outside the system will make an impact even more. In 1976, I went to work with the bomb squad. All the special units take volunteers. I had originally wanted to go to stakeout.

I had been interviewing for different jobs in the police department, and had gone in to talk to someone in vice. I really didn't like it because it involved too much deception. Undercover vice: where you get in with people, become their good 'ol buddy, and then you turn them in. I really didn't like the idea that you have to make friends with somebody and then turn around and lock them up.

I was much more interested in stakeout, which was clear-cut. You basically just go in and shoot somebody. To me, it was more clear what was happening. You want to catch the people right there as they are doing it. If it involves guns, then you are the person who has to use the gun. That was what I was good at.

That was why I was trying to get into stakeout, but their quotas were always filled up and I had to wait.

In the meantime, there was an opening in the bomb squad. This was something that I was interested in, so I went out for it. Even though I'd been in Ordnance in the military, I didn't know a lot about explosives. So I bought the technical manual on explosives and read up on it and went for the interview.

The instructor was also the head of the unit, and was the one to interview me. I knew more about it than he did. It turned out that I knew more about explosives from reading the technical manual than he did.

What I subsequently found out was that Philadelphia is a great place for on-the-job training. They were like, "We don't know anything, but we'll find out as we go along."

They sent me to Redstone Arsenal in Huntsville, Alabama, for a month of explosive-ordnance training. They called it a Hazardous Device School. That was a time when they had federal government funding, so that's why the city was so eager to bring in more people—it didn't take anything out of the city funds. There was even a rumor that what they were doing was, once you became federally funded, the feds also paid your salary, because you had to serve a couple of counties other than Philadelphia. The bomb squad would get outside calls.

It was supposed to be part of the Omnibus Act. A lot of what you heard was rumor. What I heard was that they just kept our names on the city payroll also. Our paychecks would still come from the city, so we only saw one paycheck. But that was one of the reasons, I found out later, that they put up with a lot of stuff from me—because I was a double paycheck. Instead of kicking me off, they figured they would just keep me and keep me quiet.

There was no "hazard pay" for working on the bomb squad in Philly. At the time, they just gave you your regular pay. They considered it a blessing enough that you were now in a special unit. You weren't on regular patrol.

To a large degree, this was true. Members of the bomb squad had a lot of benefits. On the downside, when the bomb squad went out on the job, the danger was doubled.

It was almost like being a fireman, to a degree. The administration decided that we were cross-trained, because we were also stakeout trained. So we wore "two hats."

My team began doing both bomb squad work and stakeouts. That became one of the biggest fights we had with administration. We wanted to be just on one specialty only.

My team ended up on details. I worked in banks and stores, waiting for someone to come in so I could shoot them. It got to be, to a large degree, a joke. We'd tell them, "Suppose we're on a stakeout job and a bomb job comes in."

Administration didn't see the problem—they told my team that they could change hats and go to the other job. This went on for about a year before administration finally gave up trying to get two jobs for the price of one out of the bomb squad.

For a while, bomb threats came in on a semiregular basis. When I originally came on the bomb squad, there were no supervisors. No one had rank. Administration decided the bomb squad needed direct supervision, so they transferred a couple of sergeants over.

One of the sergeants found a way to increase the workload. He found a provision that said that petric acid, which is a commonly used chemical, can oxidize and form crystals, which are used in explosives. The Japanese used it as one of their primary explosives.

But petric acid is also used for preserving, so college laboratories, pharmacies, and other places stored petric acid. When petric acid gets old, it forms crystals—on the lid if it's been sitting for a long time. If a person picks up the jar and shakes it or drops it, or just goes to open it, and the crystal has formed, it can explode.

My sergeant discovered this fact and began circulating flyers to everyplace that might store petric acid. We started going on jobs regularly.

To a large degree, the chance was more remote than the reality. I don't think there are any really noted cases of it really happening, but there was always the possibility. Almost like the possibility of getting struck by lightning. It has happened, but it's not a common occurrence.

The bomb squad worked on the assumption that it could happen. There were a lot of jobs on that. One job we totally ended up faking. What I mean by that is that we just exploited the danger potential and ended up evacuating a couple of blocks around the area that we were taking the petric acid out of. We had I-95 cleared for us two exits in advance so nobody would be on the highway when we were transporting it. Then we had the fire department standing by, waiting for us when we disposed of it.

This sergeant was a white guy. Our other sergeant—who is black—was a man who liked to stir things up a bit. The rumor was that when the two sergeants were in Alabama together during training, the white sergeant put a watermelon with a fuse in front of the black sergeant's door. It was kind of a subtle message that "This is going to be my thing; your thing is going to be administration. You just hang around in the office." This sergeant even told me that he went to Klan meetings while he was down in Alabama. You end up with strange friendships.

As I recall, the sergeant went to the Klan meeting as a lark. He didn't make any bones about it. He did it as a lark. That was the guy I was working for. He sat down and told me that the few people he'd shot had all been black. One day he offhandedly said, "If I was black, I wouldn't take half of what you guys do." Those were the conditions that I was working in when I was in the bomb squad. It was eye-opening, to say the least.

Bomb threats were a dime a dozen to the bomb squad, but there was one case that was particularly memorable. Somebody called in a bomb threat at the airport—Philadelphia International. The bomb squad used to be stationed at the airport because it was one of the prime targets for bomb threats. Airplanes would circle the field and touch down in an area of the airport called Cargo City. All of the luggage would be unloaded from the belly of the plane. Bomb dogs are trained the same way drug dogs are, trained to pick up unusual scents. The dog would go over the luggage and sniff it to see if there was anything suspicious in the luggage.

By the time the sixth airplane was coming in, the workers brought the dog out. The dog hit on a big box and that's when they called us in. The dog kept coming back to the box like three or four times. His handler had to pull him off of it. We figured this had to be it. We were out on the runway because this was at the end of the airport and we were outside.

The squad had portable x rays, but it was November, around the holiday season, and it was cold out there. X rays don't work if it's too cold outside.

We had to cut into the box. We had X-Acto knives. We were using those because they tell you—they create a lot of paranoia in training—a thousand different ways of setting off a bomb. Basically, if the bomber actually wants to get someone who's trying to disarm the bomb, they can set up other devices. My crew and I had to cut through layers of cardboard, slicing off each layer of cardboard one at a time to make sure that it wasn't wired. When we finally cut a hole in the box, we had to shine a light into it to see what was inside. It took us all of a half hour to cut through the box.

Just a simple box, just very carefully cutting through, taking every precaution that we could. We found clothing and then, way in the back of the box, we found a Tupperware container of liverwurst. We told the worker with the bomb dog that he needed to feed his dog in between assignments.

I was part of the bomb squad in 1985 during the siege on MOVE, a radical antigovernment group that lived in West Philly. MOVE was a back-to-nature group that preached against technology. They were protesting anything and everything. They became such a nuisance. They also stockpiled weapons and preached their philosophy to those who would listen, and even to those who didn't want to listen.

Led by a former university professor who called himself John Africa, MOVE was originally a mixed group, but primarily black. It was discovered that MOVE members were conspiring to blow up different things, and there was talk that MOVE had acquired guns and bomb-making materials.

Their neighbors complained of being harassed when they walked by, and of a terrible stench that emanated from the MOVE house, a stench that was thought to be both human and animal feces. Several neighbors witnessed MOVE members brandishing weapons, and it was said that from two o'clock in the afternoon until two or three in the morning, MOVE created a massive disturbance in the neighborhood by taking turns discussing the MOVE philosophy on a bullhorn.

On the morning of May 13, several police officers tried to serve warrants for the arrest of four MOVE members. Several shots were fired on the officers, and the police fired back. It turned into an hour and a half gun battle. Then-Police Commissioner Sambor, then-Fire Commissioner Richmond, and then-Mayor Goode agreed to drop a bomb on a gun turret and bunker that occupied the roof of the MOVE house. The bomb missed its intended target and set the entire block on fire, destroying over sixty row houses, leaving 250 people homeless, and killing eleven MOVE members, including five children.

It was not the first time MOVE and the police had tangled—there had been several other sieges in the past, one in which a police officer was killed.

By the time the bomb was dropped on MOVE's Osage Avenue residence, I was no longer with the team. I was in the firearms department. I actually requested to leave the bomb squad, finally. I ended up going to Forensics—I went to the firearms-identification unit.

Would I have helped his team drop the bomb? No, I wouldn't have done it. But my squad was the one that actually set off the bomb. It became a big controversy because they said that they had used a certain amount of explosives and a certain type of explosives in the satchel that they dropped, but the amount and type was in question. If I had been on the bomb squad that day, I would have made a big show and taken off my uniform, laid it all down, gun included, and walked off.

The MOVE fiasco is reminiscent in a lot of ways to Waco. A lot of the same questions are floating around: Did the bomb start the fire or did the people inside the building start the fire? Other rumors included the idea that some of the people, who were left inside the building as it burned, had been shot. Another allegation was that the stakeout team was in back of the building, preventing MOVE members from leaving. That rumor is because we had silent rifles, .22s. They said that supposedly every time somebody came out they were being shot at and driven back into the house that was burning.

One of my most memorable cases happened during my "two hats" year, when the bomb-squad team was doubling on stakeout. I came into the station one day, and there were stills of a security camera catching the face of someone robbing a bank. I looked at them and I said, "This looks like a guy I eat breakfast with."

My team agreed that I would go talk to the guy before someone else recognized him. I wanted to grab this guy before somebody else sees him and thinks he's John Dillinger.

I found my friend, sat down with him in a bar, and showed him the photograph. I suggested that I take my friend in, handcuffed, before someone else saw the photo and decided to shoot him. My friend looked at the picture and agreed that it looked a lot like him. "I've even got shoes like that," he said to me.

I took him in and turned him over to the detectives. The FBI was called in. An hour later, they called me back into the room. My friend told me that he did it.

What happened was that he was an insurance man. He'd go to the bars big time, drinks on the house, all this kind of stuff. He was spending the money that he was collecting. When his book came due, he just went to the bank, wrote a demand note, and got exactly the amount that he spent. I think it was $300 and some change. He wrote it on the note. I think it was $319.75, some ridiculous figure.

My friend ended up with probation, and I got a commendation for catching a bank robber. It was kind of backhanded the way I got it.

One of the jobs that made me nervous during the year of wearing two hats was when I had to sit in a bank, waiting for robbers to come in.

Part of the stakeout unit's job was to go over the crime statistics—how many robberies happened in a particular area—and out of these statistics, the unit would target areas and stake it out for potential robberies. Basically, the method was that the team would go into an area and as soon as it got hit, the word got out quickly that there were cops in that area and the robbers didn't want to hit it. Then the crime statistics went down in that area and the team would move on to another area.

A holdup at a bank involved you shooting the robbers or trying to capture them. Our primary orders were that if you shot him, it wasn't exactly a bad thing. We were supposed to be experts with firearms.

I was never taught to shoot to wound, because if you are justified in shooting, then you are justified in killing. The worse thing you could do is to try to wound somebody and end up killing them. Fortunately for bank robbers everywhere, I never had to shoot anybody.

To me, being on the police force was very reminiscent of being in the military. If somebody ordered you to take that door, take that hill, take anything, I just didn't want to do it. When I went into the bomb squad/stakeout, we were more or less on our own. We handled the job the best way we wanted to. If you felt like risking your life, you did. A lot of times, they let me be in front because I would do it. I voluntarily do almost anything if I feel like I want to do it. But I'm very order resistant. The only reason that I existed in the police department that long was that I was able to move around.

I ended up in the state parole system, in a maximum security prison. Working in the prison system had its moments, too. I ended up signing out a guy that killed a friend of mine, killed a cop. There had been a drug raid and he had shot the first cop who came up the steps. But he confessed to me that he didn't know they were police officers—he thought they were just other drug dealers that were coming to wipe him out.

I initially heard that he got thirty years, which I thought was a ridiculous sentence for killing a cop. What we didn't hear was that in the parole system, you do half of your max and you are out on parole. So he was coming out in fifteen years and I was just in the prison on parole work. When I talked to him, he told me he did five years inside the prison, then he did five years on the prison farm, which is outside the prison. After that, he did five years with furloughs, which is where you go home at least once a month on weekends. This man was a model prisoner. So when he came out of the court system and into the prison system, each system handles that occasion differently. As far as the prison was concerned, he was a perfect inmate and he deserved all the benefits of a perfect inmate. So he never did any really hard time except for the five years of jail inside.

Eventually, I was retired early, after sixteen years in the police department. I got lead poisoning when I was in ballistics because of the ventilation system. I went out initially because I was trying to get rid of the lead. I was suing the city because of health reasons. So eventually they gave me a retirement.

I sold insurance for a while. I understand that it is very, very common for former policemen to sell insurance. There is a lot of fraud in insurance.

For about five years, I put together a lifestyle-and-dating magazine for single Philadelphia residents, which I was actually doing while I was on the police force.

Then I fell in love with someone, and she told me I needed to get a steady job again. I began bodyguard work for R. J. Reynolds. I was taking people out and I was escorting them while they gave out cigarettes. They paid well. I've been privileged to see a lot of the inside of society. It isn't a pleasant sight.

I still believe that police officers are basically hired mercenaries. It isn't a popular position, but I think I have a point. What you are doing is enforcing the majority laws on a minority community. Also what you are doing is trying to keep a large number of minorities from getting in the same position that you've been "privileged" to get.

Sergeant Melvin Stokes

**Jefferson Parish, Louisiana,
Sheriff's Department**

Born in the 1940s, I grew up on the wrong side of the tracks, in north Baton Rouge near Hardin Field, at the Kirtland Air Force Base. My mom was a single parent, although I did have a stepfather who took painting work when he could get it.

Our neighborhood was rough. People were always fussing and fighting. Lots of people got shot and killed. It was so bad that during the war, when the Hardin Field base was up and running, they made our neighborhoods off-limits to the soldiers.

I was a fourteen-year-old kid heading the wrong way when I met a girl named Sylvia. She set me on the right path and, at the age of fifteen, I married her and we moved to New Orleans.

My wife made me the man that I am today.

We started our family, and I didn't have to look far for work. Sylvia's aunt worked at Charity Hospital, and got me a job in the kitchen, where I made $47.52 every two weeks. I held that job for two and a half years, then got a job working in the maintenance department of the airport. Soon after that, I worked for a furniture store, driving a truck, and then moved on to the Borden Milk Company, where I also drove a truck.

I had seen my share of prejudice before, during, and after the

Civil Rights era. I had experienced both prejudice and kindness in my life. In the fifties, my wife and kids and I took a trip through Louisiana. Our car overheated in a small town, and I was concerned about how the residents would react to a black family passing through—it could have been a bad situation for me and my family. But the kindness of strangers never ceases to amaze me. While I was waiting for the car to cool down, my family and I waited by the car. A man came out of a nearby house to find out what was happening, and I explained our situation. I will never forget the moment the man's wife came out with glasses of lemonade for my whole family.

On the other end of the spectrum, during the same trip, I went into a store in another small town to buy radiator fluid and a knife to open the can. The store owner sold me the radiator fluid but didn't want to sell a knife to a black man, even though I explained why I needed it.

Still, incidents like this didn't harden me. Instead, I tried to take these experiences and learn to understand people and why they tick. I like to think they helped me become one of the best officers to deal with juveniles in the Jefferson Parish Sheriff's Office.

It wasn't until I was in my early thirties that I took the police-officer exam. I was in this civic club, and a guy by the name of Efraim Turner told me, why don't you go take the test. The civic club had been sending black men down to take the test, but everyone was getting turned down after taking the test. I hadn't finished high school, and I didn't think my chances were too good, but I went down there anyway, and took the test. And passed. And was accepted into the police department. Turned out that most of the people who'd taken the test had something in their background—they had been arrested, or they had some kind of problem with the law, some run-in over the years. I had never had that. And so the sheriff hired me.

I was hired in 1964. Black officers in the sheriff's office didn't get to wear uniforms until 1966, when the blue-gray uniform came out and was issued to both black and white officers. Before '66, white officers had uniforms, but black officers wore white shirts and black slacks. We put our badges in the breast pockets of our shirts, and carried our guns in a holster.

Black people were not allowed to post bail for their relatives—if your son or daughter was in jail, you had to go through a civic club, talk to a white person who was sympathetic, and that white person could sign for the bond. But things were starting to change in the South—civil unrest was on the rise, and Martin Luther King Jr. was beginning to make an impression on black and white people, making them face the inequities with which they lived.

Black officers also couldn't arrest white people. They could just arrest the black people, and they were hired to patrol the black communities.

When we did make an arrest of a white person, we would have to call a white officer to transport them, 'cause we didn't want anybody to claim we did something bad to them before we got them into the jail. So a white officer would transport them, and we'd write the report on them.

The first time I ever arrested a white person, it was a speeder on Ames Boulevard, a predominantly black area. He came through there, flying, and it was about ten o'clock at night. He was driving like he was crazy, running people off the road, and everything. We gave chase, and finally when the road turned to gravel, the driver had to pull over because the gravel was so rough and he couldn't outrun us. We pulled him over, and started talking to him about what he was doing. He had been drinking, and he started cussing us and calling us niggers. Two other officers and I put the driver against his car, handcuffed him, and arrested him for speeding and being drunk. I just knew that we were gonna get some flak, but we didn't. Nobody ever said anything.

After three and a half years in the detectives' juvenile division, I was transferred to the patrol division in 1968. Although the transfer happened because several other black officers complained about being treated second-class, I didn't mind the move to patrol.

I was proud of that, the uniform, and driving a marked car. I worked there three and a half years before I talked to a supervisor about transferring back to the detective unit. At that time, I was still moonlighting for the Borden Milk Company while working my law enforcement job in the days. After turning in my application, I was transferred back to juvenile the next day. That was in 1971, and I was there up until 1996.

I like to think that if you talk to anyone in the Jefferson Parish Sheriff's Office about me, they will tell you that the department was lucky to have someone like me working in juvenile. I was good with the kids, with a knack for turning a troubled kid around.

I really enjoyed it, because I ran into a lot of kids who were off the beaten track. I shook them up; I gave them a hard time. It's a great feeling when I see somebody come up to me and speak to me and I don't even know who they are. And they say, "Man, you did this for me when I was a kid; you did that, man, I'm doin' this, I got a family, I got this that and the other." It makes me feel good. I get a lot of that.

One of the tricks I used with kids was to give them a little respect. No matter how young they were, I always called them "mister" or "miss."

I often worked detail at football and basketball games. One of the ways I kept kids out of trouble was to buy them tickets for the games. I knew the troublemakers, and in case anyone wonders if I was a soft touch, there was a motive to my philanthropy: I could see 'em better, watching 'em inside. Then I didn't have them running around outside, causing trouble.

I worked detail in a tough school in Shrewsbury, a subdivision of Jefferson Parish, in John H. Martin High School, and at first I was worried about working security there. The kids had no respect for authority, and would do anything to anyone. But when I started working detail there, I established a rapport with the kids, giving them respect, something they hadn't gotten from others. In return, I got respect from them. When there was a problem, everybody jumped on that person who was causing that problem. I didn't have to worry about it because they knew that I treated them right, they knew that I was going to do right by them.

After that detail, I took another security detail at a skating rink where no police officer, black or white, would work. There were so many problems there that it was considered to be a job similar to being placed in Siberia. But I worked the skating rink and got along with the kids.

I remember a few of the kids who came through my door and how they turned their lives around. R.L. was such a guy, a big, husky kid from Mississippi who had a chip on his shoulder. My partner and I caught R.L. out one night after the newly established midnight curfew, and we brought him back to the precinct and called his parents. The very next night, I caught R.L. again, this time with a big old knife. I confiscated the knife and read R.L. the riot act. I went down one side and up the other one. Back in the sixties and seventies, a juvenile officer had the authority to put a juvenile delinquent in jail for a short period of time. I called R.L.'s parents and discussed the idea with his father. The boy's father agreed to leave his son in jail until midnight, when he got off work. It was about nine thirty P.M. when the boy went into the tank on a weekend, and by midnight, he was scared and grateful to be out of jail. In there, R.L. encountered drunks and brawlers. He was fifteen years old at the time. It scared the piss out of him.

When R.L. got out of there at midnight, his father picked him up and told him he'd have to go back to school, or "I'll turn you back over to Mr. Stokes."

R.L. realized his dad meant business, and he went back to school, graduated, and went to work for a tool and die company, eventually making supervisor. He became a model citizen, joining the Good

Timers Sports Organization, which sponsored dances and scholarships for kids. He kept in touch with me, and always credited me with straightening him out. I remember R.L. as one of my best success stories.

Another success story involved a white teenage girl who was running wild on her family. One night, her acting out got so bad that her father, a manager in a large corporation, finally called the sheriff's department, requesting a juvenile officer. I responded.

I went to the house, and they told me what kind of problems they had, how she cut up, and how she cussed the policeman out the night before. I told the parents to bring her into the room, warning them that because she was fourteen years old, I wasn't going to treat her like a baby. She had been skipping school and hanging out with a bad crowd. The dad didn't say much. He looked at me, a black man coming into his house on a Sunday.

When her parents tried to get her to come out and talk to me, she went to the bathroom and stayed there. I stayed there for about an hour while her parents tried to coax her to come out of the bathroom. So I went and knocked on the door and said, "Either you bring your behind out here, or I'm gonna kick this door down and come in there."

When the girl told me to go away, I told her to stand back from the door because I was going to knock it down. And I smashed the door, and she come out there cussin' and carrying on. I lost it. I grabbed her and I shook her and I threw her against the wall. She come back, I hit her in the chest and knocked her against the wall again. I just knew I was going to lose my job and everything else when I realized what I had done.

I frightened the girl so much that she tried to get her mother on her side. "Mommy you're not gonna let him kill me, you're not gonna let him kill me." Her mother stayed back from the situation, telling her daughter, "Well, you listen to me. That's the juvenile officer, he's the policeman."

Man, I went down one side of her and up the other. And this guy was a big-time manager at Avondale. He knows the sheriff personally, so I said, "Lord, I know I'm gonna lose my job. I hit this girl in front of her parents."

I worried about it while I wrote up my report afterwards. I talked to her and I told her some horrible things. She done really got me teed off. She done cussed that policeman out the night before, and I told her, "You gone cuss me, I'm gone kill you. I told her, you cuss me, I'll kill you, 'cause I ain't got nothing to lose."

But there were no repercussions from the family. Five months later, I got a call from the girl's mother. Her daughter had gone back to school, hadn't missed a day, and she was graduating with honors. "I want to thank you for what you did," she told me. "Me and my husband have never hit her. Under other circumstances, maybe we would have blamed you hitting her, but she treated us so bad, we needed somebody to do something with her."

Every once in a while, I would run into the girl's mother and get an update on her daughter. She really appreciated what I did because it changed the child's life.

As for why some kids can be turned around and others can't, I think it comes down to leaders and followers. A real follower, you can turn him around, but a leader, you have to get rough with them sometimes. Still, I understand the leaders. They come from broken homes, often need to be loved but aren't sure how to reach out and get it. It's easier to find a few weaker kids and lead them into trouble. Leaders want to make an impression on people, and they use their followers to do illegal stuff like snatching purses, picking pockets, and burglary.

I also think there's too much violence on television and that today's leaders let juvenile delinquents off too easily. When I was in the juvenile unit, we locked up the troublemakers over the weekend and the JDs couldn't get out until the officer came to work on Monday night. Now, you got to call a probation officer to see if you can lock him up. You stand there looking at a kid that broke into somebody's house, or hit somebody and sent them to the hospital, and you gotta call the probation officer to see if you can put him in detention.

I've seen this overly cautious attitude with juveniles backfire. Around the holiday time, a twelve-year-old boy was in a fight, and when the fight was broken up, he was searched and several marijuana cigarettes were found on him. He'd never been in trouble before, no more than having problems at school, but they arrested the kid with these drugs on him. I called the probation officer to get permission to put the boy in a juvenile detention center.

I explained what the kid had done, but the probation officer didn't think it was enough to put him in. This kid grew up to be in more trouble than the law allows, and then he wound up being a straight-out drug dealer. The last time I heard from him, he was doing time in some eastern jail. I firmly believe that kids who have done something wrong need to deal with the consequences. This kid had never been in trouble, so if we had put him in jail then, let him know what it was all about, that would have been a turning point for him.

Some people may say that I take a hard line with these kids, but I really care about these kids and where they're headed. I want to see them turn their lives around, and I've seen the results of what consequences can do for a kid, and what can happen when a kid is let off without being charged for a minor crime.

Not all my cases had to do with turning juvenile delinquents around. There was the case of a five-year-old white girl in Louisiana who was kidnapped in the summer of 1978. We searched for her, the whole community. We had fifty FBI agents out here, and we searched.

The girl and her seven-year-old brother had been visiting with distant relatives. The man of the house came home and told the kids that they had to get out of there because he had to go to work. They left, and when her brother saw his friend on the corner, the brother took his sister's bike and left her on a street corner to go with his friend to a gym a few blocks away.

We searched the whole neighborhood for days. I got so it looked like I knew this child, I'd like to have lost my mind, because I really wanted to find out who it was.

Months later, in November, a man was hunting up in another parish, St. Charles Parish, and he ran across what looked like body parts to him. It was only a few bones and what looked like a skull, but there were clothes scattered around as well: blue sandals, eyeglasses, a polka dot skirt, and a striped blouse.

The man who discovered her had been looking for deer tracks. But after this discovery in the woods, he went home. It kept weighing on him to call the police, so he called the St. Charles Parish Sheriff's Office and told them what he had found.

When the officers investigated, it was the child who had been kidnapped from Jefferson Parish back in June. It appeared that she had been tied up and left out in the woods, because there was a rope with three loops: a big loop that would probably fit around her body, and two small loops that were probably around her arms. Evidently the abductor had tied this child up and left her there. Animals had gotten to her and her bones were scattered. The police had to go through the woods, digging around in the fallen leaves to find the bones and the rest of the evidence that would identify the little girl.

This proved to be a frustrating case, perhaps all the more frustrating because I suspected who did it, but could never prove it.

We'd like to think it was some type of ritual abduction. We found two root beer cans there, Rooty Toot root beer, a brand I've never even heard of before. There was also a Pepsi can where they found the body, but the Rooty Toot root beer cans provided the best evidence because it was probably a regional soda brand, probably an out-of-state brand.

We had a kid in the neighborhood who was a relative to the girl.

I believe the boy knew something about the little girl's abduction because the same night she disappeared, when the case was still hot, he was nowhere to be found. We talked to everybody in this neighborhood, we searched every house in this subdivision. You have to imagine the amount of homes in a subdivision: about 200 homes, 250 homes in this subdivision. We searched and we talked to everybody, including this boy.

The boy ran away that same night. I discovered that he had run away to the state of Maine, where he'd originally come from. A white investigator, one who hadn't worked the case, was sent to Maine to talk to the boy, but he lost valuable time and momentum when he realized he didn't know what to ask the boy, and by the time I was put on a speakerphone to lead the investigator up in Maine, the boy decided not to talk at all.

I'm sure that if the same case happened today, I would have been the one going to Maine to talk to the suspect.

I couldn't go back then, you know, being black. I couldn't put the pressure on him that I would have if he'd have been a black child, or if I'd have been a white officer. I'd have put pressure on and got it out of him. But I couldn't do that.

I believe that the little girl's brother knows what happened to his sister. I think deep down inside he knows. I'm close with his family. I think he knows what happened 'cause he just went off the deep end. His parents, they only had two kids, and they can't do nothing with him; he gets in trouble everywhere he goes, and he doesn't sleep at night. So he knows what happened.

I believe that we are too liberal with our kids these days. I believe that if we let them experience the consequences of their actions when they are still young and impressionable, troubled kids might still have a chance to turn their lives around.

Sometimes scaring a kid, letting them know what jail is all about while they're still young, is enough to set them on the right path.

These days, sixty-five years old and still going strong, I work with the S.T.A.R. (Survey, Target, Arrest, and Rejuvenate) Program, a community-oriented program that lets the residents get to know their law enforcement officers up close and personal. And I still spend a great deal of time talking to the youth in the community, trying to help set them on the right path.

Herbert Milton

Chicago Police Department

If I'd wanted, I could have been a movie star. I have probably given more Oscar-worthy performances than the academy gave out in the last twenty-five years. Instead, I joined the Chicago Police Department and spent fifteen years working undercover.

Anyone can do what I do, but you have to be an extraordinary actor. Being undercover means that you infiltrate whatever organization is being investigated at the time. You have to be a jack-of-all-trades. You have to know something about everything. I should be able to convince a race car driver that I've been driving race cars all my life. The secret is being able to tell the person you're investigating something that they didn't know about. You want the person to know what you're talking about, but you want to give them new information, give them the impression that you know more about the subject than they do.

I grew up on the West Side of Chicago. My family moved around a lot. We were gypsies, jumping from house to house and building to building. Almost every time my family moved, I went to a different school. The Alba homes, running from Racine to Laughlin, were my first introduction to the projects.

I think I was in high school when I got my first up-close look at uniforms. I originally had a state job in mind when I went to Career Day and met with various recruiters from the local and state departments, but it was both the military and the police department that impressed me the most.

I liked the way they carried themselves—very duty oriented, well dressed, in good physical condition. They tended to business. I knew absolutely nothing about the police other than the uniform I saw and the people I was in immediate contact with that day.

It was not until after I did my stint in the Marine Corps from 1962 to 1967, spending part of that time on an aircraft carrier that transported atom bombs and other weaponry, that I entered police work. Marines have a bond that goes beyond the job. The Marine Corps and police work are closely related. You rely on everyone around you if they're available, but you're also required to rely on yourself if there's no one there. Which is probably why, after I was discharged in 1967, I went into the police department.

I found a home in the Chicago Police Department. And, in me, the police department had found a man who had a real love for undercover work. It was a stroke of luck that I got into undercover work. A fellow officer with whom I had spent a good deal of time left the district under the guise of quitting the job. Instead, this officer moved into undercover work with the federal government. I was one of the few people who was aware of my friend's move from local to federal work because I worked with him on the Herreras case at the time. I was instrumental in helping this man with the case, and he remembered me.

It was supposed to be temporary, going undercover in my friend's place, but it lasted fifteen years. I'm pretty much self-taught. When I walked into this place, it was assumed that because of the color of my skin, I knew everything about this business. I was handed $950 and sent out to buy drugs. I had no idea what they were talking about. I didn't know how to dress or where to buy drugs. I had no idea what I was doing.

The target was a Cook County deputy sheriff. I wasn't given this information until I was standing in front of the officer, who was in full uniform with a .357 Trooper under his arm. It was a rude awakening. This situation put me in a position to trust no one under any circumstances. They schooled me very well by throwing me out there like that. My survival instincts from five years in the military came on fully and I managed to get out of the situation intact.

I shoot from the hip a lot. You only get one chance to make a mistake in undercover work.

It seems amazing, but I was never "made" during my work. The closest I ever came was a case in which I was trying to make a deal with a drug dealer one afternoon in a dimly lit sports bar. I was negotiating to buy drugs from a Latino drug dealer, and sitting to my left was a gringo and a couple of black guys. The gringo looked up and recognized me from a previous encounter. He turned to the dealer and told him, in Spanish, that I was the police. The drug dealer turned to me and related what the gringo told him. Now, I knew the bar was dark enough that if I acted quickly, I could minimize the damage.

"That's bullshit," I replied. "I did two years up in the Wisconsin State Penitentiary and just got out." To prove my point, I got up and smacked the gringo around a little bit. Since the police normally don't go around hitting people, this was a great beard for my undercover work. When the dealer and his underlings saw my treatment of the gringo, they did the same thing. In fact, they picked up the stool pigeon and threw him out of the bar. The deal continued as if nothing had happened.

My most dangerous case was the one in which I spent thirty days undercover in the Cook County Jail. My job was to find out if two Cook County sheriffs were on the take and involved in drugs. I did this disguised as a prisoner. My first day was spent in a holding cell with the other men who would be my cellmates for the duration. On my first day, I had to make a decision about what I should do.

Holding cells are large rooms that hold about thirty men at a time. All these people share a toilet, washbowl, and a water fountain. The holding cell is a small community. Most of the people in there have been there many times, and they know each other. I was new, and I was noticed right away. While I was listening to one man tell his story about stealing a six-pack of orange juice and being set up for more-serious charges, one of the head honchos walked up to me.

We had some words. He wants to know who I am and where I'm from. Now, I've got to play this by ear. If I back up too much, I've got to eat crow. If I push too hard, I've got to fight. I knew this incident would make or break me in the eyes of my fellow prisoners.

And that's what happened. In jail, you're either at one end of the food chain, or you are the food chain. We ended up trading blows, with me ultimately choking him unconscious. It had been a while since I had removed an individual in that particular way. There's a cutoff point where your body gives all the signals you need to know when to stop. I couldn't remember that point since it had been a while since I had applied those techniques.

When I realized that he was out like a light on the floor, I mumbled a few words, stood on the man's body, wiped my feet on him, and stepped down. At that moment, I was embraced by several people in the cell. They came up to me, patted me on the back, asked my name, and I was on my way from there.

Still, if events hadn't gone my way, if the guards had showed up at the wrong moment, I could have had some real problems. After I stepped off the honcho's horizontal body, the other prisoners might not have liked how the fight ended, and they might have jumped me. If one had gone for me, the rest would have followed. In that case, I didn't have any help in there. As it turned out, nobody came to the unconscious man's aid. In fact, they were eager to help me adjust to Cook County Jail life. I started to get all sorts of advice on what to watch out for, when to watch my conversation, who to stay away from, etc.

And if the guards had showed up? They would have been more likely to put a knot in my head than the other guy's. Chances were that they knew the other guy. Fortunately, he recovered before the guards came by.

The job I was given was cleaning the holding cells. I swept them out and mopped them, starting out on the top floor and working my way down with another prisoner. It was a good position to be in because it allowed me to wander around on my own to some degree. But the first two days of working in there, I thought the work was going to kill me.

Thirty days in county lockup is a long time, but it's longer if you don't know when you're getting out. In my case, I knew I would be out in thirty days. Still, there were only five people who knew I was in there, and I could have no contact with them while I was inside.

I had another close call during my time in county jail when I came face-to-face with a policeman I had been partnered with several years before. I must have aged ten years when I saw him. If he'd said the wrong thing, I would have been in trouble. Fortunately, I had a full beard as a disguise, and during my first week in there, with the work I was doing, I'd already lost seven pounds and three inches off my waist.

One of the deputy sheriffs that I was watching was moonlighting as a bodyguard for a notorious drug kingpin.

One night, this young lady came in to bond her brother out of jail. So this deputy writes her a bond and takes five hundred dollars from her. He had no authority to write that bond. He just took her money and pocketed it.

The same deputy sheriff, while riding shotgun one evening during my undercover assignment, got in a shoot-out with a rival drug dealer, and was paralyzed from the neck down. He was just doing stupid things. Now he's in a wheelchair.

During my fifteen years undercover, I can recall testifying in only four cases. I wrote reports on the others. Normally, my job can be described in these terms: I go out, talk to the suspected individuals, gather information, buy drugs or discuss drugs. I write my reports based on what was said and I quote the individual as best as I can. He's going to be given an option: He contests the information, or he can plead. The four defendants who contested the state's case now wish they had pled. The lawyers quoted my reports almost verbatim.

These days, I've gone on to work a beat car again, patrolling the Belt, the largest stretch of high-rises in the country.

When I came on the job in 1968, this was a way of life. It still is a way of life, like being in the military. It's not a job where you do your eight hours, then pack up your stuff and forget about it. I think that a lot of the new recruits look at it that way. When I look back on my fifteen years in undercover work, I consider that I did a very good job, but I don't consider my part to have been that important. Anybody could have done what I did, if they were a good actor. If not, they wouldn't be here to talk about it.

Sergeant Leonard R

Los Angeles Police Department

I was born in Pennsylvania, but moved to the southern part of Los Angeles when I was five years old. As a youngster, I held typical views of police officers. I didn't care for them too much, tried to avoid them more than anything else.

In 1965, I watched the Watts riots happening virtually outside my front door. I can clearly recall the arrival of the National Guard and the rampant looting and rioting. Compared with the 1992 riots, which took place in a more contained area, the 1965 riots extended to farther-reaching areas. Unlike the '92 riots, you didn't miss it. Everybody felt it.

However, I don't see the riots as an influencing factor in my decision to become a policeman. A larger influence in terms of awakening of consciousness was the assassination of Martin Luther King Jr. Realistically speaking, my knowledge of Dr. King really wasn't that great at that point. But I just knew that something was sorely wrong when he was assassinated and I couldn't put my finger on it. I just felt so cheated.

Instead of becoming a police officer, my aspirations were to become a doctor. I spent the first few semesters of college taking premed classes. When I was eighteen years old, I joined a cadet program with the Los Angeles Police Department. The program allowed me to work and go to school at the same time. While there, I met a nice group of friends who talked me into becoming a police officer.

I never returned to media school and have been on the force for twenty-two years, spending the bulk of my years on patrol because of my politics, except for a brief stint here and there. I have been involved in cases of gang wars, homicides, arsons, and you name it. Crime begins in a lot of places, and for a lot of different reasons. I find that some crime arises out of necessity, and some of it is due to people who have given up in life, in general. There are also the sociopaths who feed on the weak.

Crime has always been there, and as long as you have people looking to cut corners, I guess it will always be there.

I was also around with the inception of the first gangs, such as the Bloods and the Crips, in the late sixties and early seventies, when I was still in school. The murder of a man named Robert Belew at the Hollywood Palladium theater was the event that brought gangs widespread media attention. Belew was killed in a dispute over a leather jacket. But similar activity was going on earlier, when I was active in the teen post, where teens were beaten up and robbed for their coats and jackets. Even after the Belew murder, gangs weren't taken as seriously as they should have been. Because the gangs weren't a problem that impacted the children of civic and law enforcement leaders, they were ignored for too long.

It's easy to turn their backs when it's minority people killing and victimizing each other. They didn't do anything about it.

When I had been on the job a few years, in the late seventies, the police department had just opened up a gang unit named CRASH— Community Resources Against Street Hoodlums. I was working the Seventy-seventh, doing patrol work. I was working in the division they were putting the CRASH unit in. I had also grown up in the area. I knew all the gang members, had gone to school with them. And I didn't get an assignment to the unit. I just thought that was ridiculous. I had fifteen years of hardcore, firsthand knowledge of these people and the area that they could use. And the answer was no. This was racism coming out. They put a bunch of male white officers in there who had no clue where these people were, or who they were. When you complain, they say, "Quit being a troublemaker, quit being so thin-skinned. It's going to be all right. Wait your turn."

There were, however, some experiences of being a police officer that I cherish. I call the following incident one of my "jewels." I was driving down the street when I saw a little boy get hit by a car. I spent about fifteen minutes alone with the boy, then another officer arrived and the two of us gave the boy CPR until the ambulance arrived. The boy survived and I was thrilled to be able to make a positive difference in the face of tragedy. It was very rewarding.

Over the years, I have become an officer whose reputation sometimes precedes me. Some claim I have a militant view of police work, especially concerning black police officers' roles in the department.

That just goes to show that there are more people who are uninformed. I don't have a militant viewpoint. I don't know what they mean by that. I'm definitely outspoken on the issues of injustices within police work and on a lot of fronts.

Having witnessed inappropriate use of force and acts of misconduct by officers, as well as seeing some of the other concerns people have about police officers, gave me a certain motivation to become a champion of justice in my role as the president of the Oscar J. Bryant Association.

The Oscar J. Bryant Association was started in 1968 and was named for the second African-American officer killed in the line of duty in the Los Angeles Police Department's history. The first one was a guy named C. P. Williams, who, one of our historians recently discovered, was killed in 1928. The reason the Oscar J. Bryant Association in part was founded in 1968 was because of the riots in '65, and because in society as a whole, blacks were not allowed to form any kind of social group or organization. And along came the opportunity, with Oscar Joe Bryant's death, to form an organization that was nonthreatening, nonchallenging, and therefore it was an opportunity for blacks to say, okay, let's get together and do some things now that we didn't have before. We never had that chance.

The Oscar J. Bryant Association represents officers accused of misconduct and also stands up for victims of misconduct. I try to make sure that the standards of the police department are adhered to. The goal is to find the truth and try to get the truth out there. If someone was to take advantage of another person, I would simply make sure that the rules are carried out. I would make sure that if there's an issue that needs to be brought to the media's attention, that it is. If there's an issue that requires some alerting of the troops, then I do that, too.

As an example, take the case of Officer Doug Iverson, who shot a tow-truck driver. I felt it was wrong for the police department as a whole to support an effort to blame the victim, in this case a man named Daniels. What I try to do is hold us accountable. I want to set the standard for fair and ethical policing and I do that freely and voluntarily on my own.

I have been president of the Oscar J. Bryant Association since 1994 and I try to use my position to champion the rights of black officers who may not have been treated fairly within the department. We bring light to these guys who otherwise would not have a clue as to how their careers are impacted by some of the decisions that are made. I think it's wrong when people come to the job with no other purpose than to become the next chief, to try to gain more power and influence. It's wrong when we as a department take advantage of people like we do and promote the most undeserving individual around, a lot of the time. It's hard to sit back and watch that happen. No one is willing to speak up about it, but they'll sit there and complain about it. I use my position to try to gain something positive for the little guy.

I know I am disliked because of my efforts. I guess that's the bittersweet aspect of it. I've made some friends for being outspoken, and I've made some enemies. And the only thing I'm trying to do is just do the right thing. That's not always easy and that's not always popular. I'm not a militant, but I am motivated by people who take advantage of the weak and uninformed, the disadvantaged.

For these and other reasons, I have found that the Los Angeles Police Department has not been an easy place to work. They try to really shut you up if you don't toe the party line. Because I always seem to be at odds at one level or another, I've always been one of the people who've been on the outside, so to speak, of the system.

I have worked under several police chiefs in my years with the department. The first was Darryl Gates. Police officers worked under the siege mentality under Gates. It was "us against them." Police against the community. It wasn't the good guy/bad guy, it was everybody who wasn't a cop. Therefore, we had strained relationships with the average citizen on the street, which wasn't right. We had very, very poor police/citizen relationships.

After Gates was Chief Williams, who was a bit of a refresher, but a planned failure. Williams was doomed from the beginning simply because he was an outsider. Chief Williams was the perfect person to fail, and I think they designed it that way. They said, "We need somebody we can put in place, and then beat them up if we need to without there going to be a whole lot of stuff behind it." He made some mistakes and the mistakes he made were costly, but he was expendable to the system and that's the truth. I remember countless times I would tell him, "Chief, you got to be meaner, you got to be more aggressive as a chief. People just aren't going to respect you." He would laugh and say that he just wasn't that kind of person. Whatever mistakes he would have made as Willie Williams were just exacerbated. And the role of the police union was hurtful as well so he just got it from all sides.

I can still recall my first meeting with Chief Parks. It occurred in

1977, when Parks was a lieutenant. He came into the Southwest Station where I was working and that was one of the first times I saw anyone of color working in a uniform, with rank. I decided then and there that I wanted to follow in Parks' footsteps. While it takes most people fifteen years to become lieutenant, Parks had become a lieutenant in just ten years, which is nearly unheard of. I was probably naïve enough to think it was all fair and based on merit.

I didn't realize at the time just how politically connected one would have to be in order to become a lieutenant so quickly. You have to be a standout, or something has to happen for you. You got to be connected. I was just average Joe Blow. All I'd known was the police department, and the political infrastructure was all new to me.

Chief Parks has made people, the guy in the car, more professional, which is good. It's a positive step forward. Everybody is more professional, more knowledgeable because of the accountability which the chief demands, which is long overdue in the department. But Chief Parks also brings a heavy mandate as far as what he expects from his officers, not only in terms of this new accountability but particularly with this new system of discipline. He's a heavy hitter on that. It can be stifling.

Still, in comparing the department of today with the one ten years ago, it is definitely better. The department today has an agenda, where before there were criticisms that we were just floating around with no direction. That was true, but that wasn't any one person's fault. Now we have a direction and I like that.

I see Los Angeles as an important city in that a lot of things that happen in the country, good, bad, or indifferent, happen first in Los Angeles. It's a city that has a leadership role. The people of Los Angeles, as well as the Los Angeles police, need to take advantage of the opportunity to fix problems before they arise in other cities. One way to fix the problems is through community policing, which is a lot like the "broken window" concept. A broken window in a building is evidence of the attitude of the people inside. If you as a homeowner allow your windows to remain broken, it means you don't care. They built community policing around that same concept.

The "broken windows" of our communities include broken homes, drugs, lack of employment, lack of opportunity, and the closed businesses. As police officers, we need to do a better job of getting information out into the community to the people who can make the right decisions to fix all the "broken windows."

Looking to the future, police work is good for me. I've enjoyed my time here, but this is not my department. This is somebody else's department. I can't make the changes I would like to make, or do the things I would like to do. I plan to be out of law enforcement in two or three years. I have a lot of ideas and dreams I would like to follow up on. I have a nonprofit idea, like the Oscar J. Bryant Association, that would allow me to exercise some freedoms that the Oscar J. Bryant Association wouldn't, though it will be more community oriented.

I also feel I'm an entrepreneur at heart and I have some ideas where I could use my institutional knowledge. I'm also considering consulting work because I'm good with the community. Politics is also something that interests me at this point. I think we have too many people who abdicate their responsibilities in terms of giving back to the community, and I might even try to throw my hat into the ring there.

I also have concerns for the black youth of Los Angeles in terms of education. The gang issue is important, but so is general education. There are so many things missing in education that could use strong leadership, direction, and focus. The schools today simply manage mediocrity. They have you go to class and the lessons are not connected to anything that the average youth uses today, leading them to ask, why do I need that? They don't teach real life.

I'm also concerned with the media and how it influences people, especially the black youth who see few role models in the media besides sports figures. The media glamorizes the wealth and the superstars, and I maintain that that puts a lot of pressure on the youth. There is a lack of effort on the part of black youth. They try to be up there where they get all the money, all the cars, all the women, but there's no future in what they do. It's all in the here and now. If I'm able to go into education or the political arena, I would definitely work towards giving the future a meaning, instead of just focusing on the here and now.

I'll be the first to admit that I look at police work differently than a lot of other officers. I know that I always wanted to be there and to help, but I think our calling as police officers is special. It's not just going there and being the knight in shining armor, because what we do, if we do our job right, is to set people on new paths of life if given the opportunity. We're supposed to help people heal, we're the savior in a lot of regards. It's a tall order, and sometimes it's a thankless task. We have opportunities that the average person just will never have. We have access to life as it happens and we need to take those experiences and realities and derive from it the positive aspects. We need to put lessons or things in order that would help society be better.

Commander Hubert Holton (retired)

Chicago Police Department

I was born in 1923 in a small town in Mississippi—Louise, Mississippi, to be exact. My mother died when I was four years old and my father left for Chicago, leaving me to be raised by an aunt and grandfather on a farm. I attended both grammar school and high school nearby.

I joined my father in Chicago after high school and worked at his grocery store on the South Side of Chicago. At age nineteen, in 1942, I was drafted into the army. After training in Arizona and Massachusetts, I served as a military policeman. Later, I went to North Africa, to both Casablanca and Algiers, then went on to southern France.

I was on the Invasion Fleet one day after the invasion through southern France near Nice and moved on to Marseilles, where I served as a guard of installations, in hospitals and headquarters.

After that, I directed traffic in Marseilles, and also guarded and escorted prisoners to and from the front lines during World War II. In August of 1945, I returned to the United States, was honorably discharged the following November, and got married on December 29, 1945. I had met my wife through her brother, who had served with me in the service. I met her while still in the service.

During the first years of our marriage, we had three children, two daughters and a son. I worked in the family retail business until 1957, when I joined the Chicago Police Department. I actually joined the Chicago Police Department in 1955. My father sold the family business in 1957. I was in the first class of five hundred officers that were hired by Mayor Richard J. Daley. At that time, there was a small number of black police officers in the Chicago Police Department: Seven black sergeants and one black lieutenant were the entire supervisory structure of black personnel at the time I joined the force.

I was assigned to the second police district, which, at the time, was Twenty-ninth and Prairie Avenues. There were four black sergeants working in the precinct. I began as a patrol officer, working the wagon, squad car, and three-wheelers until 1963, when I took the detective exam. I was number twenty-five on the list.

I was promoted to detective immediately and assigned to a robbery unit in area two, which was located at Ninety-first and Cottage Grove. At the time, teaming up with a black policeman was on a volunteer basis. Because of my veteran status and police record, I had no problems getting partners. At first, I worked with a variety of partners, but I finally teamed up with Bill O'Brien because we kind of clicked together. The two of us made the first salt-and-pepper team in that area.

The first case I remember involved a robbery. I was doing surveillance at Sixty-second and Dorchester when I saw a person who fit the description. I detained him and recovered a weapon. This was all done single-handedly. I was supposed to be on surveillance because my partner was doing something else. But when I saw someone fitting the description, I just had to act. I knew this was the perp I'd been looking for. I couldn't wait for backup, but I did radio for help.

About a year later, I was working in the same area with a partner. My partner and I were going to a particular apartment in the Sixty-second and Kenwood area, looking for a suspect. My partner was talking with someone near the elevator when I spotted the person that we were looking for. We went into the apartment and I ended up having to fire on him. That was the only time I shot anyone on the job. The perp assaulted me, and so I drew my gun and shot the perp in the leg. I fired one shot, which just grazed his leg. I could have shot him in the chest or some other area, but I thought I could handle him. I was able to effect the arrest right there.

O'Brien and I worked as partners until I was promoted to sergeant in 1966.

After a month or so of training, I was assigned to a homicide unit in area four. I was the first black sergeant to be assigned to a homicide unit in the Chicago Police Department.

It was an interesting time, right at the heart of the Civil Rights Movement. I think I was selected to work that precinct because of my background in the military and because I was black. I supervised homicide's serious assaults and sexual-assaults investigations on the West Side of Chicago. After spending about a year in that position, I was then transferred back to area two—robbery, my old unit, at their request. It was close to my home—I lived on the South Side. That year, there was a terrific snow, and I had had enough of that travel through the old Maxwell Street Station. So I was happy for the transfer.

Back in my old stomping grounds, I served as a supervisor of robbery investigations—specifically, heavy weapons use such as shotguns, rifles, and machine guns. All of this was handled by the robbery unit. I stayed in that area and several crimes of notoriety occurred. One in particular was the killing of the eight nurses in the South Chicago Hospital. The killer was Richard Speck, a noteworthy serial killer.

Although I didn't work on it directly, I did work with the homicide unit that handled it. I also worked during the 1968 political convention. I supervised detectives at the Hilton Hotel during that era. I stayed in area two until 1972. I was then transferred to the patrol division, Second Police District at Fifty-first and Wentworth.

After a month as a patrol sergeant, I was assigned to a tactical unit in the Wentworth District which investigated the major crime incidents, including narcotics and criminal offenses. In 1979, I was promoted to lieutenant and reassigned to the Seventh District, which is Englewood District. I only worked there about four months before being transferred back to Wentworth as the tactical unit's commanding officer. The tactical units under my command conducted numerous narcotic raids. One of our cases resulted in the repealing of the no-knock rule in narcotics search-warrant cases.

A police officer had to knock on the door and announce himself before he could make entry. The no-knock case involved a sixty-five-year-old woman called Mama Connors. She used her children and grandchildren as dope peddlers. She lived in a three-flat building, three stories high, which she owned, at Thirty-sixth and South King Drive. She used Great Danes to keep the police out. When anyone would try to approach from the rear, she would turn the dogs loose on them.

On one case, we had to kill two of her dogs and we had to use some innovative measures to get into her building. We used ladders from the fire department, went through a second-floor window, because she had all the other windows barred. This is what prompted the review of this no-knock rule. Because of Mama Connors' tactics, the courts had this law repealed.

We had several successful cases against her, and we sent her to the penitentiary. I think she did something like fifteen years. The officers on my unit recovered drugs right on her bed, went through her bedroom, and discovered her with drugs on her person. As a bonus, my unit recovered a lot of stolen property that Connors had taken as payment for drugs.

My unit was the first tactical unit to successfully build a case against Mama Connors. Before that forced entry, the police had been able to make small cases against the kids she used to transport drugs, but they had never been able to get to her until I took over the tactical unit.

Also during my time in the Second District, I went up against Flukey Stokes, a big-time dope dealer. My unit successfully raided Stokes' place several times. During my eleven years in the Second District, from 1972 to 1983, my unit built a commanding reputation as a crack tactical unit. We were very successful in our operations.

Each tactical squad was headed by a sergeant and ten police officers. The tactical unit had three to four squads, and everybody worked in citizen dress. But because we worked in a confined area, it didn't take too long for most of us to become known, whether you were in citizen dress or not.

For undercover purposes, you need to be able to assemble. In fact, I had integrated staff always. It was out of necessity, because we had more white officers than we had black. Today, they have larger units and a central unit that covers the whole city, so they can bring in personnel from outside. It's easier these days to go undercover.

I got out of the narcotics investigation when I left the Second District. Back in those days, most of the narcotics were investigated by the districts. Now it is mostly centralized. We had a central narcotics, but it didn't have as much personnel working strictly narcotics at that time.

We handled it pretty good back in those days, but we didn't have the gang problems we have today. I was working the Third District, area two, during the time of the Blackstone Rangers, which was the first organized black gang. The gang was later known as El Rukns. They started around Sixty-third and Blackstone—that's how they got their name.

The Rangers started as a church youth group. Jeff Ford, who later became their leader, was about fifteen or sixteen years old at the time. I didn't know him well, but I had arrested Ford in the early days.

The Blackstone Rangers went from church youth group to gang. They had older people who got involved. But what really got them off the ground was that there was some sort of government subsidy that they got by this arrangement that they had with the church.

There was supposedly a training program of some kind. They started growing by leaps and bounds right after that.

I worked through Daley's twenty-one years in office, but wasn't promoted again until Jane Byrne, Chicago's first female mayor, came into office. In 1979, I became Lieutenant Holton.

There wasn't too much change in the police department due to the change in mayors. It was business as usual. But there was progress being made as far as black promotions. Shortly after I first came on, we had a change in the police department power structure. We had Rockford and we had the professor from California. O. W. Wilson was the superintendent during my time. After Jane Byrne, we had Brezack. I served under him.

In 1983, Representative Harold Washington became Chicago's first black mayor. Fred Reist was named head of the department. I was promoted to commander. I was assigned to area two, Detective Division, where I had worked some twenty years prior as a detective.

Area two was where I started my career as a detective in 1963. In 1983, when I became a commander of that division, I supervised from 130 to 150 police officers, including lieutenants, sergeants, and detectives. My division investigated violent crimes and property crimes in the Fourth, Fifth, and Twenty-second Districts, all on the South Side of Chicago.

Surprisingly, there was very little resentment for a black veteran who had risen in the department. I was known by some of the detectives from my own years as a detective, and word got around that I was an all-right person, a no-nonsense type—though there were times when I had to use my charm to get compliance. I was successful at that.

Perhaps it was because I was a veteran, a no-nonsense man who played by the rules and treated everyone fairly, but I can't recall any outright racial discrimination as a police officer. I had a good career on the Chicago Police Department. I had good relations with white and black, Hispanics and all.

My first case as commander of area two in 1983 happened the very first day I was on the job. I was called out at four in the morning. There had been a triple homicide at Ninety-first and Ashland Avenue. It was a drug party and two brothers had killed three people. We had them under arrest by eight in the morning.

My detectives got a lucky break—one of the people in the building where the homicides had occurred knew one of the people who frequented the apartment where the three people had been killed. That got us a name. We were able to get one of the brothers and he snitched on the other one. We were able to round them up rather quickly.

I was also responsible for cleaning up my department. Charges of brutality, including a well-publicized case of a lieutenant in my department who had been prosecuted for police brutality right before I took over, were becoming more common. My area was known for brutality. I successfully stopped the aggravations of brutality in that area during my time.

How did I clean up my department? I did it by being present. I made frequent inspections and I let them know that I would not tolerate any brutality. I let them know that I would not accept it under any circumstances.

I served in that capacity from 1983 until 1986, when I turned sixty-three years old. Chicago has a rule that after age sixty-three, you cannot serve in an exempt position.

But I remained on the job another two years, then I retired in 1988. In all the years I was on the job, I never had to fire on a suspect. I'm proud of that record. I had persons who worked for me who had to kill people in their line of duty. I had one police officer who was shot while under my command. That was the only one out of the many cases that we handled—particularly serving search warrants, crashing doors, only one police officer was shot.

By this time, my son, Hugh, was well entrenched in the police department. In fact, it took Hugh only four years to make detective, rising fast in the department. A sergeant in six years, and he made lieutenant shortly after I did in 1981. In 1983, Hugh was promoted to exempt rank; my son and I served in the exempt rank together. It was the first time in the Chicago Police Department that any father and son had served in an exempt position at the same time.

My daughters went different ways, although one did attend the police academy, only to decide that police work was not for her. One daughter became a teacher, and the other is in the computer-science industry.

One grandson, Aaron Holton, is now a detective in the narcotics division.

I put in thirty-three years of service in the Chicago Police Department. Despite my retirement, I went back to work after nine months of rest. I played golf and traveled, enjoyed life, but then we had a long winter and I went out looking for a job.

I was hired by the inspector general of the Chicago Housing Authority and began work in March of 1989, serving as chief investigator, then deputy inspector general, and finally as inspector general, until retiring a second time in 1996.

Captain Commander Hugh Holton (deceased)

Chicago Police Department

If you're going to do something, do it and do it well, or don't do it at all."

This is an attitude that was passed from my grandfather to his father and on down to me.

I remember playing football in high school for Mount Carmel. At one point I wanted to transfer to another school because I thought I would have more playing time. My father sat me down and explained, rather bluntly, that he didn't send me to this exclusive Catholic boys' high school to play football and that I was going to stay there. If I never played football again, it didn't matter. I was going to finish at Carmel, which I did.

In 1956, when I was ten years old, my father joined the Chicago Police Department. But having a father who was a police officer didn't heavily influence my decision to join the force. It wasn't a conscious idea that I can recall, that I wanted to be a police officer. But it was something that was always in my mind.

While nearing the end of my high school years, I began to look for ways to pay for college. I was hoping for a scholarship, but I found the Police Cadet Program. The program had been recently implemented and "encouraged young men between the ages of seventeen and nineteen to take the job as police cadet and it would provide money for college." I kind of fell into it that way. It was more a matter of convenience.

I graduated from Mount Carmel High School on May 31, 1964, and started with the police department on July 1.

My duties as a police cadet were mainly administrative. I spent almost two years as a cadet before enlisting in the army. As a cadet, I knew officers who were going out to the antiwar demonstrations and riots in their robin's-egg-blue helmets and other riot gear, but I was never exposed to that. Instead, my desire to enlist was due more to another deep-seated family value.

We have had a member of my family in every war that we know of going back to the First World War. And my nephew was a navy reserve in the Gulf War. No one ever said to me, "Well, you have to go and do your duty and go to Vietnam." It was just what was expected. It was seen as something that we do. There was never any question. I never would have said I didn't want to go. Maybe patriotism is outdated now, but I guess that's the best word.

I enlisted in February 1966 and got out in December 1968, spending the last eight months in Vietnam.

I was in the Veterinary Corp, and then I got into something called the Civic Action Program. We would go out to the villages— there were only a couple of us—and we would assist the Vietnamese people by vaccinating their animals. We had an officer with us that helped them construct pig farms. It was a strange program. Vietnam was a strange experience altogether.

One of purposes of the Civic Action Program was to promote goodwill, and while the Vietnamese accepted our presence and our help, we did get fired upon once. No one was hurt, but they were sending us a little message.

After my experiences as a cadet, I knew that on my return from Vietnam I would become a police officer. That was my sole intention as my choice of occupation. When I knew I was going to Vietnam, I discovered that I could take certain phases of the prescreening selection process. And since I was in the military, I could put a waiver on the process and take different phases as time permitted. I took the written exam in January 1968 while home on leave from training in San Francisco. Then, before I left for Vietnam, I took my physical. When I came back from Vietnam in December 1968, I took the waiver off. I was back. So it only took until March 3, 1969, for me to be hired. I was on the fast track that way. I wasn't wasting any time.

As a police officer, I was first assigned to the Nineteenth District, which is on the North Side of the city, not far from Lake Shore Drive and includes Wrigleyville, the area surrounding Wrigley Field, home of the Chicago Cubs. The area was semiexclusive at the time, with a few depressed areas, such as the Kenmore area.

One of my first experiences had to do with a very large Native American who was picking fights with people in a bar. I was assigned to a field-training officer, and we were assigned to back up another officer who was working alone on a case. We had this three-hundred-pound man picking fights and knocking people down. A big person can be very difficult to handle.

When we walked in, he couldn't care less about us. We had to fight him. I remember him throwing a beer bottle at me and it shattered. I remember actually using some football stuff. I tackled him. I pulled his legs out from under him. He went down on the bar floor with a very, very loud smacking noise, like he did a belly flop. He didn't think I would do it. Once he was down, we knew he wasn't getting up. We handcuffed him and took him out.

After working in the Nineteenth District for a year and a half, I transferred to the Second District. The Nineteenth was something of a slow district. Except for the uptown area, there wasn't a lot of crime, and it is still a fairly exclusive area. I wanted to get into a faster-paced operation. The Second District has a very high crime rate. Lots of public housing, lots of gangs, lots of drugs—then as it is now.

I went to the Second District to work plainclothes tactical. It's not undercover. It's anti–street crimes. You see guys walking around with jeans and big guns and bulletproof vests on. That's what we did.

As far as working undercover, I'd done it only one day for a couple of hours. I had gone to testify at the trial of an individual I'd arrested for attempted murder of a police officer, criminal sexual assault, a number of things. I was giving testimony. I kind of dressed up for it at the time. I was kind of well turned out. When I walked into the station, they kind of ragged me a little. I was the youngest officer on the tactical team at the time, and my partner said I looked ideal for helping clean up a prostitution-streetwalk area, so they were going to send me out there.

"You look like Little Lord Fauntleroy," he said. Out I went, and I was amazed. One of the prostitutes actually said she knew me from working plainclothes. She said it was unfair of me to come out there dressed like that, because I fooled them. Usually, they send someone that they can kind of recognize, but me, I looked like a total mark to them.

I took advantage of every possible opportunity within the department, and from working plainclothes tactical, I was promoted to detective. I also qualified by written examination to be an evidence technician—an officer who would go to the crime scenes and collect evidence. But I ended up taking the detective position and worked with youth crimes. I did that for three years and was promoted to sergeant. Every opportunity that ever came up, I tried to take advantage of it. I know people who are content to stay right where they are, but I wanted more. I became a sergeant when I was twenty-eight years old. At the time, I was one of the youngest in the academy. It took me eight years from that point to make lieutenant, simply because they didn't give any examinations during that period.

When I became a commander, my father, who was still with the force, was also a commander. We were the only father and son in the history of the department to be commanders at the same time.

Of the thirty years I was with the department, twenty-five of them have been in a supervisory position. It forced me to work alone if I was on the street, primarily. I had a number of partners, but I never had the luxury of developing a close personal relationship with a partner because of the nature of the assignments I've had, being a sergeant, a lieutenant, and a commander.

Despite my one-day stint as an undercover officer, I had little inclination to work undercover again. I want them to know when I walk in the door that I'm a cop. That fact alone won't make me immune from anything bad happening, but I would rather be in a position of recognizable authority.

My personal confidence has contributed to my success as a supervisor. I've got to make them believe that what I'm telling them to do is the right thing and that we're not running a democracy. Sometimes you have to say, you will do it because I said, "Do it." In other words, because of my training and education, you will do what I tell you to do. That's the kind of supervisor I am. I have a saying when people say, "Can I ask you something? You may know this." I say, "If it's important, I know it; if it's not important, I won't."

I think my officers feel confident that I know what I'm doing, and they will come to me for advice. Once they ask for my opinion, it becomes an order that they carry out.

I demand respect from other officers, not only for myself but for fellow officers. I don't care what you think of me as an individual or what you think of my race. But if I've got that lieutenant's bar on and I'm sitting in the watch commander's office with the watch commander, you are going to respect me, or I'm going to try to fire you. I'm not trying to work out your problems. This is pretty much the way that the Chicago Police Department handles it. Leave your prejudices at home. Don't bring them to work.

In a similar vein, I remember when female officers first came to patrol in the middle 1970s and a male officer attempted to refuse to work with them.

This guy said, "I don't work with females." So I said, "Then go home. This is a job. You didn't volunteer to do this. You can't come in here and tell me who you will and will not work with. That is out of the question. This is a professional operation. If you are going to have a problem racially or with a person's sex or with their sexual preference, then what is going to happen when you get out on the street and we can't see you?" I don't tolerate it. I'm very, very blunt about that.

While women were hired on police forces as long ago as the 1880s, they were hired mainly as matrons to handle female prisoners. It wasn't until the mid-1970s that women were hired as patrolling officers.

There are a lot of tragic situations. We lost three officers in the last year. One of them was shot to death in the district I work in. The other was shot to death right on the border of the district I work in. Still there has to be humor to temper the tragedy. It's not uncommon to laugh at roll call and to laugh about situations that occur.

One officer, Joe Davenport, was having problems with a masked figure dressed like Zorro coming into the station and attacking him with a sword:

It didn't hurt him, but he's the only one who has seen this person. It's kind of a joke. We ask him, "Why are you the only one who sees Zorro?" It's a little thing to lighten things up. We also have a homeless person who comes into the station. The first time he came in, he saw me and he claimed to the desk that I was his cousin. I went to see him and I said, "I'm not related to you." He said, "Well, okay, I thought I could try." After that, when I'd see him, I'd yell at him, "I told you about coming in here. You're going to embarrass the whole family."

Aside from the humor, what keeps my enthusiasm for the job is keeping abreast of new technologies, including DNA typing. I also take advantage of every possible opportunity to include the educational aspects of police work, and ended up getting a master's degree. There is so much to learn I will never be able to stay with the department long enough to see it all. New cases, too, keep the work exciting and urgent. I look forward to it every day. It's continuously interesting, and you know you are contributing something.

With a job that is continuously interesting, I've had no trouble finding topics for my novels. However, I use little from my experiences in my books. The fiction I write is pretty much from my own imagination.

I did use the story of the fight-picking Native American in one book, but only as a cameo. The book, *Violent Crimes,* featured an area in the Nineteenth District. The area, known as Uptown, was ethnically diverse—Appalachians, whites, Native Americans, blacks—with a high crime rate. During one patrol, I found a baby alligator in the street. It was pretty good-sized. It wasn't one you would find in a pet store.

Being a fiction writer, however, can be as problematic as being a police officer.

People are always asking me, "Did you put me in the books?" As far as police officers, I have a pretty standard line with them. I say, "Well, have you read the books?" They say no. I say, "Well, go out and read them all. Tell me who you think you are."

One time, two officers nearly came to blows over the character Blacky Silvestri, both claiming to be the officer on whom Blacky is based. I went to a retirement party and both officers were there, unbeknownst to me. They were discussing my books, and one said, "Guess what? I'm Blacky Silvestri." The other guy said, "You're not Blacky Silvestri. I'm Blacky Silvestri." Later I found out they almost came to blows over this. They confronted me on the telephone and pretty much what I said is, "Well, Blacky is a composite. I took the best of both of you and I made him Blacky Silvestri." That satisfied them to a certain extent.

Fiction writers have more power than police officers as well. I've gotten a lot of flack from cops when I killed a character who was very popular, to the point that I ended up bringing him back to life.

Reggie Stanton and his brother ended up being brought back from being killed in the third book, *Chicago Blues*, to make a resurgence in the fifth book, *Red Lightning*. My editor, agent, and I looked at it and I didn't say Reggie was definitely dead. I said my character Larry shot him.

It's kind of fun being a cop and a writer at the same time. People come in and ask if I'm the writer. They ask if they can bring in my book so I can sign it. I'll do that. There have been a few who would like to get into writing, and one officer, after she wrote her book, got represented by my agent and is being published now.

Officer Florida Bradstreet

New Orleans Sheriff's Department

I grew up in the city of New Orleans. I was born in 1942 and raised with two other siblings. My father died when I was seven years old, and my mother worked to support the family. My brother and sister and I went to school. My childhood was full of dull, boring routines, and I was a delicate little child, overly protected by my brother and sister. My mother was a very, very strong, very religious black woman. They don't make 'em like that anymore. Even though she was at work and she couldn't watch us twenty-four hours, seven days a week, she did. I think she had little spies out to watch us if we'd get outside and do something we weren't supposed to. She always managed to find out.

At the age of sixteen, I decided that I was grown up enough to get married. The marriage was not altogether happy, and it ended after eleven months. I married a second time, and this time, it lasted.

In the mid-1960s, the police department was predominantly white and male. At the time, I had become an activist with CORE, a civil-rights group that staged sit-ins and worked to promote voter registration among black citizens.

I can recall on Canal and Rampart, they had an F. W. Woolworth there. We were doin' a little sit-in demonstration just to be able to buy a hamburger at the lunch counter. I had to be about fourteen or fifteen. We just did our little sit-ins. We were beaten, kicked, set on. Look, that's another story right there I could go into.

But while I organized sit-ins and worked on black people obtaining the same rights as whites, I thought on it, and in the early 1970s announced my desire to become a police officer. Having led a sheltered life, it came as a huge surprise when I suddenly announced that I wanted to become a police officer.

Everyone looked at me like I had lost my last mind.

My mother told me that she would disown me. My husband put his foot down, absolutely, positively, no, no. It's too dangerous out there. Like I said, I had been sheltered all my life. I never knew what it was really like to go without, if you can understand what I'm saying. But here I am announcing I want to be a cop.

My desire to become a police officer came from witnessing so much injustice at the time. I saw so many things that I thought I could change, meaning the way that I saw some of my black friends being treated or their kids being treated. To me, it just didn't seem that it should be that way. I often saw my friends being pulled over by the police for no reason other than the fact they had black skin, and that didn't sit well with me.

After the shock wore off around me, I tried out for the police department. In my heart and in my mind—I was young then—I always felt I could do anything I wanted to. I've always felt that way.

I had to go through a polygraph test, and several physical requirements. I had the right height because I'm five feet six and a half inches, but I failed the polygraph. You never can guess what I failed the polygraph on? When I gave my complete name, he said my name was not Florida Bradstreet. The machine registered that I was lying about my name. I really became frustrated. I thought they were doing everything they could to keep women from joining the force.

There were a handful of women on the force at the time, and I didn't make the cut. But I did make the grade as a deputy for the New

Orleans Parish Criminal Sheriff's Office. Now that was very interesting. I worked there for approximately eight years. Now, that was an experience in my life that I would really love to write a book about.

I worked as a female guard in the parish jail system. I saw all types of physical abuse perpetrated by the deputies onto the inmates. I saw homosexuality, and beating the inmates. I actually saw women raping women. It was something in my mind that I just could not erase. I feel that a lot of people in the jail who were awaiting trial were innocent until proven guilty but were not treated that way. Being locked down and having your freedom taken away can do a lot of things to you. Even though I make a lot of arrests, I still believe when you go to court, the final decision rests upon the jury.

In the jail system, I witnessed a lot of corruption, inmates persuading deputies to bring contraband into the jail. Contraband can be anything. It can be bar soap, drugs, money, letters, weapons, anything that isn't permissible.

Eight years later, I transferred from the New Orleans Parish to Jefferson Parish and moved up the ladder. While I took a five-hundred-dollar reduction in pay, working conditions were better. I could come home and take care of my family, 'cause I was only working eight hours, while in Orleans Parish I was working twelve.

In the meantime, I had had numerous miscarriages and my husband and I adopted a six-week-old boy. As if that wasn't enough, my husband and I became foster parents. My son said he wanted a playmate, and I knew I couldn't give him a sibling, so I got him a playmate. I became a foster mom.

Over the years, I've taken in a total of twenty-seven foster kids. They've all turned out beautiful. Some of them are in the military, married, grown and gone. Some of them I can't get rid of, they still come by.

During the time I was with Jefferson Parish, I finally got a chance to attend the academy. While I was there, I worked full-time, from six A.M. until two P.M. The academy classes began at six P.M. and lasted until ten P.M. As if that weren't enough, my husband had a heart attack and had to have a six-way bypass.

My husband's in the hospital with open-heart surgery. I'm between my day job, gettin' off, runnin' to the hospital to check on him right quickly, home to check on the boys, get ready for school at night, get out of school, run back to the hospital to check on him, and I would spend the night there, leave the boys home, return back to work at six A.M. It was a full schedule.

That was a long time in my life, but I managed to graduate the top of the class. I don't know how I did it, it had to be the Lord. Got the academic award for the highest average in the class. Then I went on the street, patrolled the street for Jefferson Parish. I loved it, it was so beautiful.

In my first days on foot patrol in Jefferson Parish, I encountered a lot of teenagers who should have been in school. They were cutting class, skippin' out of school, breaking into houses. So I started leaning on them a lot until I got the nickname "the mean bitch."

I patrolled the streets of Jefferson Parish for three years before one of the supervisors with the detective bureau began to suggest to me that I become a detective. He'd apparently been watching the reports that I'd been writing, but to be honest, I enjoyed the streets, even though it was dangerous. Believe me, there were moments.

Those moments happened mainly when I checked empty buildings in the warehouse district. We were single, main units, going on a burglar-alarm call at two or three in the morning. My scariest moment came when I answered one of the burglar-alarm calls. I checked the outer perimeters of the building and discovered two guys trying to break into the warehouse at the rear of the building.

Now, some officers would assist you. If they weren't tied up on a call they would come and back you up. But a lot of times we didn't have that, so you would have to go in by yourself and check.

Fortunately at that time, I had a backup unit. One of the male officers went back there and dealt with the situation.

You know, a woman—I don't care if she's in uniform with a 9-mm on her side—she still has the fear of being raped. I believe that could have happened to me that night. In my mind, I believe I could have been hurt by those two guys that night.

And that was what made up my mind to become a detective. Once I made the move to detective, I began to realize the dream I'd had back in the seventies. I was assigned to the Personal Violence Unit, in which I investigate child abuse, sexual abuse, domestic abuse, and rape. I discovered that I had a God-given talent for obtaining confessions without beating the suspect into admission. I can sit down and talk with someone over and over, for hours, and they will eventually admit to what they are being accused of.

I can pick up immediately whether someone is being truthful or not about the details of an incident. My technique is to interview the victim first. When you take a five- or six-year-old child, those are the most honest people that you can ever meet. But a five- or six-year-old can lie, too. It's not an intentional lie, it's a lie that's been planted in them by someone for whatever reason.

A lot of times, the lies stem from a child-custody dispute. The mother will prompt the child to say that the father or uncle did something to him or her.

The child will give the right answers to the wrong questions, because they never know what questions will be asked until they sit in there.

Then I meet with the accused. I recall a case in which a twenty-seven-year-old male had sexual intercourse with a seven-year-old girl. The little girl was very, very credible. I got the guy in, who happens to be the mom's boyfriend, and he denied having sex with this kid.

But a doctor had examined the child and it was clear that her hymen had been broken by intercourse. There were positive findings that she had prior sexual intercourse.

I talked to the suspect for thirty minutes before getting a

confession. I just told him, "Look, I know what happened. She came on to you. Let me tell you, those seven- and eight-year-olds want to have sex, they just have to."

I went on to sweet talk the suspect. "I can imagine that she came up to you and told you she wanted to have sex." The suspect agreed, and was relieved to have someone who understood his position.

I went further to get his confession—I told him that when I was nine years old, I was "so hot, you touch me, I'd burn your hand." The suspect was eager to confess by the time I got through with him. He was proud of what he'd done.

When they admit to having sexual relations with a kid, it makes me so nauseous, it makes me just want to do anything I can to that person. But for some reason I can't curse them, I can't yell at them, I really can't get angry with them face-to-face. I just had that feeling inside of, you know, this is revolting, you need to really be in jail.

I recall one fellow telling me, "Man, when you be smokin' that crack cocaine and drinkin' that Cisco, it makes you do things that you can't think about."

Well, why fool with it if you don't have control over yourself? I have a guy in here right now doin' forty years for havin' sex with his six-year-old daughter because he had gotten that Cisco—that's a wine—and was smokin' that crack. And he comes home and has sex with his daughter, his six-year-old daughter.

The mother found out about it, and when we got there, the mother was sitting on the coffee table with a long butcher knife in her hand, waiting to kill her husband. She wasn't giving it up to nobody. If anybody had tried to take it away from her, she was going to kill them. When the father walked through the door, she was going to use it on him, and any one of us who tried to prevent her from killing him, she was going to kill them.

We eventually got the knife away from the woman, and every year, the woman makes a little cake for my birthday and brings it to the investigations bureau. Her husband is in jail right now. She has six children, and without a dad being in the home the kids are really giving her problems. One of her sons, she has brought him to the investigations bureau and ask that we talk to him.

One of my strengths is the ability to talk to teenagers, especially boys. My friend, and now the supervisor in charge of the S.T.A.R. Program, Lieutenant Renee Washington, has worked together for many years with troubled teens. Washington has more of an affinity with girls, so between us, we make a formidable team.

Say if you were here in Louisiana and you had a teen kid that had been giving you problems, or havin' difficulties in school with their peers, or whatever, you would call the investigations bureau to report this. We'll tell you, "Well, bring that child over here. We'll see if we can talk to him." And we have really been successful, talking with teenagers. That they have contacted us and brought report cards to show us that they've straightened up, they're getting good grades now, that's a positive thing that I can say she and I have as a team.

My success at getting confessions is probably because many of the suspects look upon me as a mother figure. Once I gain their trust, I get their parents' permission to be alone with the teen. I always like to say to the parents, "Look, you know when you were young there were a lot of things you did that you didn't want your mom to know about. But we really need to get to the truth as to what really happened. I think maybe they'll tell me if you're not in the room because a lot of kids don't want to see that disapproval in their parents' eyes."

A lot of the parents won't leave, but that's all right, I get the confession anyway.

I also believe I succeed in confessions where others fail because I'm a black woman. A white male officer trying to interrogate a black male suspect, it never works. Once you have placed that black male in a position where he feels subservient to the officer, he's not going to give you anything.

Oftentimes, I'm called from home or during my vacation time to come into an interrogation situation. Successful interrogation depends on the white officer, how experienced he is and how street-wise the suspect is.

I have been trying for years to get the department to send me to a school for interrogation techniques, but so far, I haven't been successful.

They say they don't want me to lose this talent that I have. I mean, I'm doin' this without having acquired that knowledge, textbook knowledge on interviewing and interrogating suspects. One case involved a young man who had just gotten out of jail two months earlier. He was creating havoc in Jefferson Parish. He was raping women like they were going out of style.

I caught him by sheer accident. I had just returned to duty after a stroke, which resulted in emphysema. I had been put on light duty, mainly office work. The officers who had picked the suspect up had put him in the office with me while they cleared up some paperwork. The suspect had been advised of his rights.

To pass the time, and because I am basically a friendly person, I struck up a conversation with the suspect. So I said, "Boy, it looks like you're in some trouble, huh?"

The suspect agreed and used a string of obscenities. "People trying to tell me I'm a rapist," he said. "Man, I didn't have to rape no second woman."

I kept the conversation going. "Last time I checked, I was a woman. Kindly watch your mouth."

"Ma'am, I'm sorry," the boy replied.

"That's all right, boy. What the hell they got you in here for?"

"I told you, the cop said I raped some woman," the suspect repeated.

"Well, did ya?"

"Hell, no."

"They must think you did," I pointed out, " 'cause they got you in here." The conversation continued, and within an hour, the suspect admitted to raping five women, and he admitted to raping one woman who had told the officers that she wasn't raped.

So, I went back to the officers who'd hauled in the suspect and repeated what had been told to me, including the victim who had said that she wasn't raped. The suspect went to trial and ended up being sentenced to 460 years.

I later went back to my fellow officers and told them I knew that they had set me up with him because they knew I couldn't do much talking with my emphysema.

I think that's human nature. When you did something wrong, you really want to talk about it to someone.

Sometimes whatever magic I have as an interviewer doesn't work. In one case, there was a serial rapist in Matairie. The perp was black and only raped young black women, then burglarized their homes.

This was when Renee [Lieutenant Washington] and I used to work together. Renee was at one time my protégée. I call her a walking encyclopedia.

Prior to determining that they had a serial rapist, I had developed two cases in the same area with the same MO. One day, I was talking to Renee, who was my supervisor, and Washington noticed that there were several other rape cases with the same MO in other areas.

The two of us talked to other investigators in the section, and gathered other cases. We were assigned to investigate. Needless to say, I wanted to kill her. So Renee said, "Don't worry about it. We're going to go out, and we're going to solve this."

We canvassed the neighborhoods, showing a police sketch of the rapist to potential witnesses. Normally there are more than just two investigators who do the canvassing, but in this case, it was just us, going door to door with nearly a thousand houses in the immediate vicinity.

We did our canvassing after our normal duty, putting in long hours. We talked with everyone. We talked with crooks, we interrupted drug transactions, we walked that area. Renee even talked to stones; Renee could talk to anybody. If it's immobile long enough to listen to her, she'll talk to it. Rocks, walls, anything. So it was getting to be like two o'clock in the morning, we both were tired. We came across several young teenagers that really should have been inside.

The kids were fascinated by encountering two policewomen. They got into a conversation about it with us and asked us what we were doing in the area. So we told them.

"Oh, you all lookin' for the rapist," one teen said. "Well, he's in jail."

"So how do you know?" I asked.

The teens went on to tell us why they thought the suspect was the rapist.

We filed the information away and went on with our canvassing. We were getting ready to call it a night when I suggested that we check on the man whose name came up with the teens.

We were both tired, but we went to the lockup anyway, and found the suspect in question. One of the descriptions from the victims was that the rapist had the name A.J. tattooed on his left hand.

Bingo, we caught him. He was now identified. Renee and I went on to check out another piece of information that would positively identify him: One of the victims had recently had her apartment broken into and she had just purchased a gun. After the perp raped her, he took the gun when he burglarized her apartment.

On the arrest report, I discovered that the suspect now in jail had had that same gun on him when he was caught.

The legwork had paid off, but what we really wanted was a confession. We talked to him, and we talked to him. He didn't want to talk to me because he was afraid to talk to me. But he did talk to Renee Washington.

He didn't trust me, you see, 'cause I look wicked. Well, we surmised the fact that apparently in his mind he knew that he would confess to me, so he didn't want to confess at all. Therefore, he didn't want to talk to me.

The sheriff tried to make a deal with the suspect if he confessed, but in this case, it didn't happen. It was just something about me that, we surmised that he knew that I would get him. He wouldn't admit to anything.

We hit the pavement and talked to people. At this point, the department wanted to help Renee and me. They wanted to give us all the help we needed.

And we said the only thing we wanted was for them to back off and let Renee and me handle this. Sometimes blacks do better talking to blacks. You can extract more information if it's a black on black, talkin' to black people in the community.

But do you know, we got a conviction on him.

I was one of the four officers who worked on getting Project S.T.A. R. Program going. Originally, I was to be a team member, but then I became sick with emphysema. You do a lot of walkin', talkin' with people, and with the emphysema, I couldn't do the walkin'. I left the position open for someone else who could do the walking, and stayed with the Personal Violence Unit. Also, it would have been hard for me to leave my position in the unit. I am currently the only black woman on the job, and I believe I have proven myself invaluable to them.

My job affords me an opportunity to try and reach these kids out there. That is one of the reasons I am so grateful for my job to be able to reach some of these kids. And to me it's worth it, it's worth it.

Officer Derrick Armstrong

Chicago Police Department

I grew up on the North Side of Chicago. I went to a public school, played football and ran track. I grew up in a family with strong moral values. After I graduated from high school, I went on to join the Marine Corps. That was in 1968. I went to Vietnam, but was fortunate enough to not be stationed on the hill.

I see a direct correlation between the sports I played in high school, the military, and my later police work. Coming out of high-school sports, running track and playing football, you depend on team members for the success of the team. It had nothing do to with whether you were black or white, you were a team. The person who usually has the best qualifications as a quarterback is the quarterback. The best catcher is the wide receiver. The best guard is the guard. You are taught how to play with the team.

When I went into the service, I was taught the same thing. It had nothing to do with anyone's color. You are no longer black or white. You are all green. You are a team. I'm not saying there is no racial overtone when you go into the military, but during wartime, it doesn't take very long for those attitudes to blow away. You begin to realize that this white guy and this black guy might be the difference between me staying here and me going home. I've got to put that racism aside. Military combat has a way of doing that. It's the same way in football. If I've got a racial problem with someone and I'm a halfback, and I have to go through a hole that the guard has got to open up for me and we have a racial problem, he may not open that hole for me and I'll be running into a brick wall. So you have to put those attitudes aside and work as a team.

When I got out of the service, I looked for employment. Jobs were scarce in the early 1970s, and I found myself dropping applications all over the city. I heard the usual, "If anything becomes available, we'll call you back." I was given first consideration as a veteran, but no one was calling to offer me a job.

Then one day, an employer was looking over my application and said something that shook me up. He told me that the only thing I had a good background in was sports and being in the martial arts and the military, because I had dealt with rifles. In joking with me, he made a comment that I would be an ideal good choice for the mafia as a hit man. My response to him was that I thought I was the wrong nationality.

But I went home to think about it. I think that might have had some influence—my background leans that way. The only other thing I could do was to return to active duty in the service. I think that with every little boy's childhood, when you go and play cops and robbers, you want to be the police. I had looked up to police officers when I was growing up, and law enforcement began to look like a viable option to doing more time in the service.

In the early seventies, jobs were not only hard to come by, but most veterans had a difficult time adjusting to society after their war experiences. A lot of the returning vets had gone into the service in order to avoid a jail term. They came out doing a minimum of two years and they had a vocation. It made things a little rougher as far as what type of lifestyle or vocation you wanted to choose. If you had no job skills, the only thing you knew how to do was pick up a rifle.

Employers were giving away five- and ten-point bonuses for returning veterans when an employment test was taken. Eventually, I ended up attending the police academy and taking a job with the Chicago Police Department. My skills with weapons did not go unnoticed, and after serving my stint on patrol, I was brought onto the hostage/terrorist team, where I spent fifteen years.

Finding a common denominator has been what makes me such a successful team player, and a leader. One such example happened during my years with the heavy-weapons team. I was working with a white guy and I happened to be the only black when I worked on the midnight shift. There were thirteen of us.

One night I had to stop all pickups and equipment, and my partner was an officer who lived in a predominately all-white area of Chicago called Bridgeport. As we passed further south of the projects, the neighborhoods started to look a little better. The homes were a little better taken care of, the lawns were manicured, the residents made a little more money so they could afford a little bit better neighborhood.

As we got off the expressway, and started for my home, I noticed that he was really eyeballing the homes that we were passing by. Then he asked me, "Where are we going?"

I replied, "Home."

His next question was, "Do you live over here?"

I said, "Yes, where did you think I lived?"

To my amazement—and I respected him for it—he said, "You know, I don't really want to sound stupid, but the only blacks that I have ever really had any contact with have been the blacks we have worked with on the job and the ones we lined up." I was the first black man whose house the white officer had ever been to, and he admitted that he had nothing to compare it to. He only had a preconceived idea, which he had been taught as a kid growing up.

You have a lot of that on this job. You've got a lot of whites in that same category. They don't know anything about blacks other than what they see at work.

Unfortunately, when the police officers go on a call to someone's house, they don't see anything but the negative. That is the only time the police are called, when something bad is happening. I think that as a whole, personally, that blacks have an opportunity to see things a lot clearer than whites, because we know the good. We've seen what happens to those who are successful and where they go and we all want those good things, but unfortunately because of the times we didn't always have those opportunities.

In recent years, with education and opportunities, black men and women now have those doors opened for them. And I know there are poor white people, too, in certain areas of Chicago. But even when you do have whites in the poor, they don't admit to being poor and don't act like they're poor. Now, if you go down to Kentucky or Tennessee, you have a different situation. But in big cities, whites tend to think that they are different.

These days, I teach classes that tear down these myths and try to reach inside a person to get them to deal with their real feelings and with the realities of what life is and is not, so that they can see things equally, without any prejudices. The class is invaluable in helping officers understand situations as individual, and not as stereotypical.

As a rule, I have been pretty successful. I have had a case where I have had a diehard who just refused to accept what I'm saying. I've had a couple incidents where I've been called on by name, not in a direct way but unconsciously, where you might be talking in general terms and someone may slip and say something derogatory and someone else catches it. You either act like you don't hear it, if it's a slip, or you see it as something becoming commonplace.

In my class, I like to use the example of a minority officer becoming a team member on a unit where the other members aren't used to Hispanics or blacks on the team. They are accustomed to talking as if you aren't there. And so when you are there, they don't pay any attention to you, because this is what they have been doing for years. You have to decide, "At what point do I correct them and let them know that I am present and I am human?"

A minority officer who is having a problem [should] refrain from speaking in a negative or derogatory manner around the other members, but instead demand as a person, not as a black man, the other officers give him or her the same respect that they would want to be given. Sometimes it works out where you don't have a problem. Occasionally you will run into that one person where it does become a problem and you might have to take it to the boss. Hopefully, your boss is intelligent enough to see what is going on and handle it in the right way.

I've been lucky, knock on wood, in taking racial problems to my bosses. I've had bosses who didn't hunch their shoulders. I've had one incident where the supervisor used to like to tell racial jokes. I felt they were being done for my purpose, being the only black. Every time I heard them, I was there. I spoke to him about it, and he took offense. I asked him not to do it in my presence, because that is the way they were being done. I thought they were being done in very poor taste.

The supervisor didn't want to hear that his racial jokes were offensive, and it got vocal. He told me that I was off the team. Well, that wasn't a problem. I'll still get paid eight hours a day, whether I'm working as an officer or whether I work blue-and-white. So that wasn't a big thing to me, because I earn my pay when I come to work. As long as I can look in the mirror and I can see pride with what I see and I am content with what I see, that's all that matters.

I took the situation to my boss the next morning, and the issue was discussed. I was asked if there was anyone who could back it up. I told my boss that everybody on the team was aware of it, but whether or not they would say anything, I couldn't be sure. I would like to think that over the years I've developed a rapport with the team and I'm not just the token black.

As it turned out, in a few days the boss called me and told me that the other team members had supported my complaint. The supervisor had been transferred. We've got some good bosses on the job. I'm not going to say that they are all good; we've got some who turn a deaf ear.

Most of the cases I worked involved domestic situations in which the husband took his family hostage while the hostage team negotiated with him for what could turn out to be hours at a time. Usually, the perpetrator had too many pressures built up—losing a job, marriage on the rocks, too many bills to pay.

The hostage team is called in to negotiate and, if necessary, take out the threat to the family. Often, the unit members must keep in mind that they shouldn't consider any situation too routine to stay alert. They must never become lax in the way they handle a situation.

In a hostage situation, there are several hours of standoff. Often they can be talked out of it; other times they end up giving up. For the most part, the hostage situations are all domestic related. Every now and then you might get one where someone might have committed a robbery of some sort and fled. After several hours of negotiations, you wear him down. Again, they surrender themselves.

It's a routine you can get used to after a while. It's routine in the sense that you drill and train and you know what to do and you follow the procedures. It's like going out on patrol, you know what you're supposed to do and you do it.

But it's the first time that you think that you don't have to do something, that it's just routine, you become complacent. You become lax and you make mistakes. You have to bear in mind that you are up against an unknown element. You don't know what he knows, or what he has or where he's been, so you have to handle each one of these like it's the real thing. That is the only way that you can come out always on top.

I look at each situation as a danger, a time when it could be my last day, when I might not come home, in order to keep myself on top of the situation at hand. It's a matter of priorities. Some people look at things where it gets to be the same old routine thing.

I see the perpetrator in a hostage situation as someone who could be me, my neighbor, or a family member. Most of the people who end up taking their family hostage have had the same situation happen to them over and over again, and they have done everything they can to get out of the difficulty. But they just can't seem to shed themselves of the problems. It can be overwhelming. We've all had bad days, problems at home, sick kids, financial difficulties. I don't like to prejudge. That's just the way I am.

Becoming overconfident or lax can also happen if you're on the bomb squad. If an officer deals with bombs every day, he or she handles a thousand cases and none of them have really been real or anything, after a while the officer can develop a complacency. But there is a danger to that—it can cost an officer his life. You always have to think positive: "I want to go home. I have a family to go home to. I have a life beyond the police department, so how seriously should I take this?"

It bothers me and many other officers who work in this unit that there is no hazard pay with the Chicago Police Department. It is a voluntary program. Lots of us have argued about it over the years.

But Chicago's argument for not instilling hazard pay is that the city officials would have reason to demand certain expectations of the people who volunteer for the program. But when it is strictly a volunteer program and anyone can apply, it depends on who you know or what color your skin is. It allows for any- and everybody to come in, and people don't take it as seriously. We've been very fortunate that we have never really had a bad situation in this city. If a really bad situation does occur, the volunteers for the hazardous units won't be as prepared as they could be with special training.

One of my skills was the martial-art training I received in karate. I was accepted into the police academy and went through the training, but once I got out on the street, I found out that a lot of traditional karate, per se, was not really practical for what law enforcement did, which was basically constraint and control. I then began to look into other forms of martial arts. Aikido was a martial art with practical defensive techniques.

I also had the opportunity, from my work in martial arts, to travel to Tokyo and study the forms that the police department uses over there. I did a little studying and my interest was in what the Tokyo Police Department was doing as opposed to most of the other people. My traveling companions were a lot younger than me and they were more interested in karate in general and how Asians train as opposed to Americans.

I began to study under a good friend who taught aikido. Having studied with the Tokyo Police Department gave me some direction. My independent research paid off. I now teach defensive techniques, using a blend of aikido and jujitsu, which I call "aikjitsu," and gearing it toward law enforcement needs.

I am a teacher of both the physical and the spiritual. I am able to teach recruits submission holds and how to retrain their thinking regarding racial and class issues.

As a training officer, I always tell people—the recruits that I train now—never underestimate the other guy, because he may not be well educated or maybe he is poor, or whatever his social/economical conditions. You don't know where he's been or what he's done. You are getting a five-minute dissertation on a background that may be leaving out pertinent elements about this person. If you run in with a preconceived notion or idea about something, you could be blown out the door. I don't think that is what I got paid to do. I certainly don't think they pay me enough money to give up my life for that.

I have also taught a rape-awareness class with the American Red Cross. When I first came onto the force, there weren't many female officers on the street. There were no grief-crisis counselors to call. There wasn't a female officer that you could call. You had to tactfully interview this rape victim on your own till you could get them to the hospital and possibly through the assistance of the nurse have her assist you in trying to collect whatever information you could get. I have a very strong moral stance on the issue, and have the men and women in the class take a poll, giving them different situations and getting their responses. The men usually find their answers and the right answers to be surprisingly different.

A lot of the men who attended were spouses or boyfriends or brothers of a lot of our rape victims. In polling the group, I always ask, as a general scenario, if all of you have dated and you've been in this kind of situation. How many times have you been in that situation when a girl has told you no that you stopped? They all look around at each other. Maybe one or two will raise their hands. Then I'll ask the next question—how would you feel if someone did that to one of your loved ones, your mother, your sister, your daughter? Everybody becomes hostile and agitated. That isn't what they wanted to hear. I said, what's the difference between when you did it and when they do it? There is no difference.

Whether I am talking about race or sex, a lot of men follow their family traditions and moral values. A lot of it has to do with home. My father always told me when I was doing the rape program that I have a mother, I have a sister, and I have a daughter. I wouldn't want anyone to put their hands on them in a violent manner. As a matter of fact, I remember telling my sister and her fiancé, when they announced their engagement, that if at any time you feel compelled or feel on the edge that you are likely to strike out, call me. I'll come get my sister or you can put her on a train or plane and I'll pick up the fare. But don't you put your hands on her. I told him, because you have a mother and you have a daughter and you have a sister as well. And if I was having an affair with any one of them, you wouldn't want me putting my hands on them. My opinions aren't always popular. For instance, I believe that people coming onto the force should be at least twenty-five years old. When you come on at twenty-one, although legally you can vote, you can drink, you can buy weapons, so forth, the average person has never really lived as an adult, and in most cases they are still living at home with their parents.

Most twenty-one-year-olds have just recently finished college or, for whatever reasons, didn't finish. Now, all of a sudden, you get trained, somebody puts a badge on you and they tell you to raise your hand, and they are going to tell you that you have all this God-given power. You walk into a person's home, under a domestic, and they are old enough to be your parents. If you were raised properly, to respect people, it is an awkward feeling to be twenty-one, twenty-two years old and to walk into a person's home who is fifty-some years old and take charge and tell them what they are going to do, what they have to do, and consequently what you will do if they don't follow your directions.

It is an uncomfortable feeling. I have noticed that a number of young recruits have problems handling awkward situations like that.

To be a good policeman, I think it's not just so much carrying a gun, chasing cars and bad guys, but a lot of it deals with people skills, how to talk to people, dealing with a domestic-battery victim.

As a training officer these days, I teach recruits the basics. To become an instructor, you had to have a basic course and then you go on to an instructor level course.

To be recertified, other training officers and I have to go in and be retrained every three to five years just so we can keep up with the changes in the law.

With defensive tactics, as opposed to straight martial arts, there are certain considerations that we have to be aware of, such as, you always want to make sure the technique will work. Secondly, as a police officer, you have to be concerned with the legal ramifications. If someone jumps out of the bushes at you, you are going to deck him and take off. You may not even report it unless you think you may have been a victim in some way. The third consideration that we have to be concerned with are the morality issues. I can use one technique, which can get the job done, and I can also use another technique, which will get the job done, but it may leave permanent damage. So which one is the better choice of the two? These are things that we have to look at.

One of the problems that the administration is trying to correct is the way some of the recruits are being trained once the classes are over and they go on patrol. The reserve of knowledgeable officers who are willing to be teamed with a new recruit is low. The reason there is a shortage in training officers is that everybody wants to be a tag man—wear plainclothes, drive an unmarked car, and wear blue jeans to work.

By the time a rookie gets three years on the job, if they're not already on tag, they're putting in for tag or are trying to get out of a district and go to a specialized unit like gangs, narcotics, prostitution, intelligence, or wherever.

What ends up happening is that the officers who end up doing the training either don't have a lot of time on the job and are left in the pool, or you get veteran officers who are coming back into the district who, as we say, have been there, done that.

But what ultimately happens is when a lot of older officers come back to the patrol division, they don't want to be bothered with teaching anybody. They don't want that responsibility. I'm not interested in wearing blue jeans and chasing people and jumping fences and doing all those wild things I did twenty-some years ago. All I want to do now is come to work for eight hours, try to do it good, and go home to my family in the same condition, the same way I came to work. I'm not interested in proving nothing to nobody because I've done that already. My record, my career speaks for itself.

Carolyn Armstrong

Chicago Police Department

I grew up in Chicago, living mostly on the South Side. I had a two-parent family and a sister. After finishing high school, I attended college for a couple of years. Before going into police work, I worked as a secretary at the Sears Tower.

Thirteen years ago, my mother called me at work and told me that there was an ad in the paper—they were taking applications for the police force. So I ran down to city hall and put in my application. In August, my application was accepted, and I went into the police academy for four months of training. There was a lot of physical work. I felt like an old person in the class because I was thirty years old and the majority of the class was in their early twenties. Still, I had gone to aerobics, so the physical work wasn't as grueling as it might have been.

Which was a good thing. During my days on patrol, I had a female partner, and it was like there was a fight every weekend. We would always be challenged. We just did what we had to do. It was kind of crazy. If you've got to fight, you've got to fight.

Despite some of the more physical aspects of the job, I see my job as being more of a social worker or a counselor. We are called in to restore peace and mediate in most cases, especially domestics.

A lot of people put the emphasis on carrying the gun when you're a police officer. But how many people actually have to use it? I've never had to. But I have had to use my whip. I've occasionally had to use some force to calm down a suspect. The gun makes them want to sit down and listen. But as far as using it on someone, no, I haven't had to. The physical end of it, sure, I may occasionally have a person who wants to give me a hard time, especially if you are female. But more often, I find that humor works better. Joking with the suspect and getting down to his level gets him to see reason a lot more quickly than force.

We are taught basic fighting skills in the academy. Pressure points are very useful for women officers. I like the wrist and the nose. Those are my favorites.

I had a partner once who was six-foot-four and 240 pounds. When we came on the scene, it was like, "Yes, sir, whatever you want, sir." If it was just me, the suspect wouldn't want to do anything I asked. You'd just have to look at him and it's like, "Whatever you say, Officer." The only problem was that he liked to keep the windows down. We'd freeze in that car. But other than that, Willie was a character, too. It was a lot of fun. I've had good partners and that also is a plus.

Quite a few women who came on the job came in around the same time I did. The attitude toward women was different even twelve or thirteen years ago. "Women can't do this or that." "What are you going to do when you are trying to arrest a man and he won't let you arrest him? You are going to have a hard time." "Men aren't always going to be there to help you."

The negative attitude in the classroom didn't deter me from going into police work. It got to me sometimes, but I know my potential. There were a couple of goofs in the class, but I handled it by remembering that there were things that I would excel at.

Negative attitudes toward being black didn't happen very often to me when I was on the police force. The only time I remember my race affecting my work was when I was on patrol, working with the public.

A woman told me I needed to go back to where I came from. She happened to be from Baghdad. I thought that was funny. My partner was of Japanese descent, so the woman told us both to go back to where we came from. We both laughed so hard, we couldn't stop laughing. I don't think she got it. You've always got to find the humor. There is always something funny. You have to find the humor.

I spent three years on patrol before I took the detective's exam. In 1990, three years after beginning police work, I became a detective. I was assigned to the Violent Crimes Unit. A day in the Violent Crimes Unit in Chicago starts with the preliminary investigation, which is handled by the car patrol that is first assigned. Once they've got as much information as possible, they notify the detective division. A team of detectives is sent out, depending on what type of case it is. Normally it would be whoever was up first that day. The watch commander will tell you, "Okay, you're up. You've got this." So you go out to the scene, talk to the preliminary investigator, and find out what they've got. Then you start working from there.

In most cases, it's an unknown offender. Or sometimes I would only get a nickname. You have to go out and canvass, find people who possibly witnessed it, and that was probably the hardest job. Getting people to say that they saw something is not that easy.

Most witnesses don't want to talk because of fear of getting involved and the fear that if they spoke up, someone would come after them. I worked with a good trainer who taught me how to talk to witnesses, to get them to say what they saw. I learned a lot from him. Basically people want to talk. They really do. You just have to say something that they can relate to. Once the witness feels more secure, the interviewer can get them to talk.

Suspects want to talk as well. When one of us brings in a suspect, we go straight to the interrogation room. Usually more than one detective talks to the suspect, taking turns with him or her.

A police officer doesn't want to go into an interview with a suspect until he or she has something concrete to use against him. I often let a suspect know that I knew what he knew. In fact, I often led the suspect to believe that I knew more than he did.

Another tactic often used was to play one suspect against the other. In most cases, both perps wanted to talk, which I found surprising. Basically, people want to confess.

My first murder case—the one I felt I'd worked from the beginning with my partner—was a case where a man was kicked to death. There were about twenty witnesses on the scene, standing by in the street while the victim was killed. By the time the police got there, they had all scattered. The only thing that was left was this guy who went to the hospital. He didn't die immediately—he stayed in a coma for three days before he expired.

Then we got the case. We had no witnesses. All we had is a body in the hospital.

I started where most detectives begin when they have a cold case—with the family. I tried to find out where he was last seen, who he had last been with. Gathering information led my partner and me to an abandoned gas station where the victim used to hang out and drink. We questioned a guy the victim had supposedly been there with. He was real reluctant, *real* reluctant. It was like pulling teeth.

Finally, he mentioned the fight between the defendant and another guy. All we got from him was the nickname of the suspect, but he did mention several other people who had been there. We had to talk to I don't know how many people.

We finally got some folks who admitted that they had been there and that they had seen what was happening. But all they had was a nickname, too. One of the witnesses told us that he'd seen the suspect take his car to a nearby auto shop to have it fixed that same day.

He was able to identify the kind of car the suspect had, and we went over to the garage to find out if a car like that had been brought in, and who it belonged to. The garage attendant was able to tell us that the car belonged to a woman who happened to be the girlfriend of the suspect who killed the victim. We went to her house, but he wasn't there.

We talked to the girlfriend, and she told us her boyfriend would be back later. When we came back later, the suspect knew my partner from working the street. My partner had been on the street for about twenty-five years. We sat around. We ate Kentucky Fried Chicken and chatted. He didn't know the guy had died. We're talking and my partner said, "You know why we're here."

"Probably about that fight I got in," said the suspect.

We asked the suspect if he wanted to go down to the station and talk to us. There was no problem with that. When we got him in the car, I advised him of his rights. At that point, we told him that the guy had died. The first thing he said was, "You mean a guy can die just from being kicked and stomped?"

We had solved the case within ten hours of it being assigned to us.

I felt good about that one. I think he felt remorse. I don't think it was his intention that it would go that far. But it happened, and he handled it like that. We had to respect him for that. That case was a lot of footwork, a lot of witnesses who didn't really want to be witnesses. But I remember having a good feeling when the family came back and thanked my partner and me for solving the case.

One of the weirdest cases I ever worked on was a very high-profile case that involved a guy who was shooting hookers with a bow and arrow.

It was a very cold night when my partner and I got a call about a woman who had been shot by a bow and arrow. The arrow went straight through, like in a cowboy movie when the arrow is sticking out the front and the little feathery things stick out the back. The victim was running down the street, trying to flag down people to help her. Unfortunately, she was in an area where there wasn't much trust.

My partner and I didn't see the arrow right away. We had to drive by slowly to get a good look at her. In that area, even we thought twice before getting out of the car to approach someone who looked to be in need of help. There had been several times police officers had been ambushed by a setup like that. But when we finally spotted the arrow sticking out of the victim, we called an ambulance.

There had been quite a few victims in that same area where the woman had been shot, plus he had gotten quite a few in the south suburbs. Although the victims hadn't died yet, this one did expire, and the charge went from aggravated battery to homicide.

The bow that the suspect was shooting the victims with had a scope on it, so he could be quite accurate. It also made it difficult to find witnesses who actually saw him. The victims never saw him coming. They were usually just standing, working their corners. Next thing they know, there's an arrow sticking in some part of their bodies.

Quite a few detectives were assigned to work the case. My partner and I, we weren't going to quit till we found a witness who had actually seen the homicide. I think it was quite a while before we found our witness.

Two other detectives who were working on it were checking out other angles. They were going into the suburbs to see what they could find out. After my partner and I found a witness who gave us a description of the suspect, the other two detectives found an archery place that remembered selling the type of arrows that were being used to a man who fit the description. Soon after that, everything began to fall into place. My partner and I found a witness who was able to give us more information on the suspect. Working in conjunction with another jurisdiction, we were able to arrest him.

I still remember one thing the suspect said after he was arrested: "Who's going to believe a couple of hookers over me?"

He was a real nut case. He was crazy.

He was paranoid, too. I was the only officer he would talk to. He didn't trust anyone else. He didn't want anyone to bring him anything—if someone offered him a can of soda, he thought it was injected with poison. In fact, he wouldn't stand in a lineup, because he had on his prison outfit. We were either going to have to put everyone in the same outfit, or give him something that would cover up the prison jumper so the witnesses wouldn't be able to tell that he was an inmate. I finally talked him into wearing this old sweater. He was a real piece of work. In fact, he defended himself. And lost.

I cleared up quite a few crimes. I worked on a lot of interesting homicide cases and I had some good partners. We did some good work.

My favorite case would probably be the one where I met my husband, Derrick Armstrong. Although I can't recall the assignment offhand, I do remember butting heads with my soon-to-be husband.

When we first met, it was tense. I was a new sergeant. I called for a car to handle an assignment, and the dispatchers assigned him. I didn't know him from Adam. I could tell from the response I got from the other officers who were on the scene that it wasn't going to be easy. "Oh no, that's Derrick."

I wondered who this Derrick was who was upsetting the other officers. I found out soon enough. I sat in the car, waiting for him, and when he arrived, he came over to the car. I could tell from his attitude that he wasn't pleased with getting the assignment. He suggested that possibly it could have been handled another way. I just held my ground. I told him it was his assignment. You could see the fumes coming from his nose. He stomped off. For the next couple of weeks, I was public enemy number one. After that, he came around to my way of thinking.

His partner could tell me stories—eight hours in a car with Derrick talking about me. At the wedding that was one of the things he got up and spoke about. A lot of people were surprised. As far as being married to another police officer, we complement each other. He knows I'm not going to stand for much. He's a marine. Once a marine, always a marine.

There's been some glamour on the job as well. For a short while, I was the inspiration for a television show about two female police officers. It didn't last long, but I enjoyed the fame while it lasted. The production crew came to Chicago to get some different ideas. They interviewed a lot of people in the area, and became interested in my partner and me. We were supposed to go to dinner with them, but we could never get our times together. I guess after speaking to some of our coworkers, they decided to put her in high heels with a purse and that was supposed to be me. My partner at the time was Polish.

Robin Givens played a detective. She wore high heels and always carried her purse. That was supposed to be me. She had a Polish partner. But the show didn't last.

These days, I'm a sergeant, and I spend much of my time supervising. I do roll call, give the other officers their assignments. I also go out there and pitch in when needed. It's a break from a high-crime area to primarily an office job. The area I'm responsible for is the airport. We provide some security and we also do traffic control. I've got civilians working for me who are primarily responsible for traffic and the officers rotate back and forth between security for the airport and assisting the traffic.

Although I wouldn't object to a transfer, it's not that easy once an officer becomes a supervisor. If you want to move someplace else, someone would have to want to come to where you are at. It has to be an even switch. I'm in a pretty good spot now. I'll be here for a while, unless I get lucky and make lieutenant.

Still, I do miss the detective division. You get a lot of respect. But being a supervisor is a totally different world. I've done this for four and a half years. I just don't feel like I'm doing as much as I was before, giving as much.

But once a sergeant accepts a supervisory position, he or she can't go back. I hope that someday I'll be able to go back to the detective division as a supervisor, but those jobs are hard to come by.

But with my relatively new marriage, a sixteen-year-old son, and two grown stepchildren, lighter duties are fine with me right now. I don't like bringing the work home with me. The "police" side I show out to the public, I don't want to bring home to my son. If I have to use certain language, if I have to get hard, I don't bring that home. I never bring that home. The way you respond is pretty much dictated by the way you are approached. It's just part of the job.

I'm also finding the time to go back to school. Actually I always wanted to get into law, but I'm not too crazy about school.

I've got about ten more credit hours before I get my degree. I just want to get my bachelor's—twenty years later. I wasn't mature enough when I got out of high school to appreciate it. When you pay for it yourself, that's when you appreciate it.

Officer Michael Ballard

Chicago Police Department

Sometimes people don't always figure out what they want to do until they fall into a profession. That was the case with me. I kicked around for about ten years, doing jobs that allowed me to work outside. I worked as a mail carrier, then as a pipe fitter in construction. But I didn't like that. It's hard work, and it's seasonal. Not many buildings being built in the winter.

By the age of twenty-eight, I was working as a computer specialist for the *Chicago Tribune*. I was the supervisor with a crew of eight, but I missed working outside and found the job too tedious for my tastes. The department was taking applications, and a friend of mine was going to apply, so I went with him.

A year later, they called me and asked me to go through the academy.

By the time I came on the police force, I'd had five or six other jobs, and had been both just an employee and a supervisor. When I got to this job, I was more settled, more seasoned. The training I went through at the academy couldn't prepare me for the real hands-on work on the police force. When you're at the academy, it's all book knowledge. I think that may have come from having instructors in the academy too long. Especially if they've been in the academy teaching for ten to twelve years; they're teaching what happened ten to twelve years ago. I think they have a course for the instructors where they come out on the street now and then for a week. Re-grouping and getting in touch with what's really going on out here. But this is something I think they just started recently.

It was also a little hard for me at the age of twenty-eight to be-come an employee again. I'd had a supervisory position at the *Tri-bune,* and suddenly I'm not in charge anymore.

But it became rewarding work, and I turned out to be good at what I did. I began in July 1982 and have seen a lot of changes in those seventeen years. Back then, the police force consisted mostly of white men. They did not like the idea of women or minorities on the force. But now women and minorities must be accepted. They are your partners every day. Those problems do still arise, however, be-tween the male and female officers. Some men on the force say that female officers are reluctant to respond to calls unless they come from other female officers. When you're new, straight out of the academy, you get that help from the female cops, but after that, for-get it. I currently work foot patrol on Forty-seventh Street. It's some-thing else, Forty-seventh Street. Prostitutes and narcotics. It's very entertaining out there. I've been out there walking for about five or six years now. Plus, it's not too far from where I grew up.

The hours I work are better than in the past and I like the foot patrol. It's not a lot of ripping and running up and down the street, going from this call to that call.

Being a police officer carries some heavy responsibilities. Once I got this job, I've been unable to keep up certain associations with people from my past since I often see people I know and went to school with. Everything they're doing, you can't do. Everybody's getting high or doing other things you don't want to know about.

Being a police officer can also put stress on the officer's personal life. I don't think many women can handle being a policeman's wife. It's a hard job, because of the hours, because of the stress and the things that go on in the streets. It's hard to come home and talk about your job because I don't think the people at home can relate to the problems out in the street you have to deal with. Every time a cop is needed, something bad is happening. Nobody calls 911 and says to tell Officer Bob to stop by and have a cup of coffee later if he's not doing anything. Every time they call 911, it's a problem, and this problem has to be resolved or fixed one way or another.

All those problems add up to a lot of stress, which can put a strain on any relationship. A police officer must also be more careful in his personal life or he may lose his job. If I get into an argument with my wife, we don't fight, or I go to jail and lose my job. Now, everyone else, if they do it, they get a court case and go to court, but it won't affect their job.

Before working foot patrol, I trained recruits for several years and was a plainclothes officer for five or six years. I see myself as having mellowed over the years. When I was a rookie cop, I did everything by the book. There was no doubt that all traffic stopped for me. You're gonna have your seat belt on, you're gonna make proper left turns, or your license is not affixed properly. I would write tickets for everything. Now I see it more as a money game that the city plays. And that's from years of going to traffic court.

The difference between the citations that I once issued and the ones that I issue now is, depending on which branch of the traffic court you're in, it's a game, it's the fine, it's the money. If I load someone up with eight tickets, half of them are thrown away in traffic court, anyway. So you may not have had a new-issued sticker on your license plate but you have it in the glove compartment. When you get to court they're gonna throw the ticket away because you'll bring them the sticker and show them, yeah, I have the sticker, I had it at that particular time when the officer stopped me but I had not put it on the vehicle. And then at that time the judge will say okay, but those tickets are already thrown out and then that was a waste of my time writing it. So nowadays I don't go through those chains anymore, I don't waste my time with those trivial tickets I know they're probably gonna throw it anyway. And they have what they call hazardous and nonhazardous movements. Hazardous is red lights and stop signs and things of that nature. Nonhazardous are citations for your seat belt or headlight missing.

When it comes down to giving the officer credit for a good job he's done, it's the same thing. They have hazardous and nonhazardous tickets that are basically like the parking tickets, so, depending on when you check off in the evening, they want to know how many citations you've written, how many arrests you've made, and they have two boxes on them for the tickets one if it's hazardous and one if it's nonhazardous. The hazardous tickets are the ones that the officer gets more credit for; the nonhazardous tickets are considered like parking tickets. So at this point now, if you want to look like, for instance, a young officer who wants to go into plainclothes with gang crimes or something of that nature, they're gonna look more aggressive on paper if they have more arrests and more citations issued. So the more tickets they write, the better they're gonna look, compared to the nonhazardous or the parking tickets. The officer's efficiency depends on how their ticket writing is graded.

And the ticket writing is a way for the inspector to tell how the officer is performing every day. The amount of time you take off, the days that you miss from work, your attendance. Are you prompt? Are you there every day on time? We have inspectors out there checking us, and they want to know how many times the inspectors have stopped you and written you up for different violations. All this stuff is included and they put it on your efficiency, which is, I think, like for every six months. While some officers are headed for bigger and better things, some abuse their power.

I had one former partner when he was a member of the tactical unit. We were in the same class. We came on the job together. When all three classes were asked who we wanted to work with when we got out onto the streets, he was the one officer everybody liked. This former partner, however, ended up in jail for accepting money from drug dealers in return for protection. It was amazing.

At the time the investigation started, I had been assigned a new partner, so two officers under investigation would be put together. Though I was unaware of the other officer's dealings, it dawned on me when I recalled the time I spent with my partner trying to catch a drug dealer. The drug dealer would bring drugs in for others to sell. We would come in about four or five in the morning to catch him. My partner told me that the drug dealer would come in early in the morning and drop off the drugs in an abandoned car. The dealer who distributed it on the street would wait a couple hours to make sure no one was watching and then retrieve the drugs about seven in the morning.

We had all this information, and we could never get this guy. I just couldn't figure out why. After all this hit the fan, I was like, no wonder.

As the former partner of the offending officer, the FBI interviewed me as part of the investigation. I was allowed to listen to a few of the tapes made by the other officers. One officer said he wouldn't try to give me the money. "He would have dropped it anyway."

Another time, I refused to accept money after a gambling raid. One of the guys tried that once. He said, "Your cut's in the drawer." Unsure of what the officer meant, I opened the drawer, saw the envelope, closed the drawer again, and left the office.

Besides trying to capture drug dealers, I have been involved in many emergency situations. One that sticks out in my mind the most was when my partner and I were driving around and spotted a building on fire at Forty-seventh and King Drive. The first floor was the home of a barbecue restaurant, which is where the fire started. The upper floors consisted of apartments. The owner of the restaurant was out front and told me that there were a lot of people on the upper three floors.

I went into the building, knocking on doors and telling people to vacate the building. On the fourth floor, I found the apartment of an old woman who had her television volume turned up so high, she couldn't hear the smoke alarm outside her door. I finally got her attention and she opened the door to me. I carried her down the stairs on my back, while the smoke became thicker and hotter. By the time we got down to the second floor, I almost couldn't see my hand in front of my face. In the dense smoke, I lost all sense of direction and had trouble breathing. My partner had told members of the tactical team that had arrived that I was still in the building. The tactical-team members guided me out of the building by shining flashlights through the smoke and calling my name. We succeeded in getting the woman out of the burning building and [she] was sent to the hospital for smoke inhalation.

I saw the woman about three months later, and she was doing fine, so that was the good part about it. Everybody got out of there safely with no casualties. We even got the cash register out of the barbecue place.

Another benefit of the experience for me: The experience helped me quit smoking cigarettes.

I am a police officer who brought many different job experiences to his police work. But being a police officer is the job that stuck with me. And once on the force, I have accumulated experience in many and varied roles.

I've done it all. There's nothing else that I haven't done. So it's comforting to know I can do anything.

Arnie Stewart

Washington, D.C., Metro Police

I grew up in the northeast section of Washington, D.C. A single mother in a working-class environment raised me and my sister.

I actually grew up in an extended family, my grandmother, aunts, and uncles. We were poor, so I knew that there were limitations. Even though I don't think I could have articulated it then, I knew that we just didn't have a lot of things. That was always clear to me.

My mother provided a good role model—she provided for her children by working hard to better herself and pay the rent. My mother went to school, worked a full-time job, had a part-time job cleaning houses, and sold Avon products. She was very busy.

From my early childhood, my aspirations ran to law school. I always wanted to be a lawyer. That was always my aspiration, to go to law school. My sister wanted to be a doctor, and we had a sort of bargain with each other that we would follow our dreams.

I graduated from high school in 1981 and attended the University of Maryland, but the environment was racially different and academically challenging. I had gone to an all-black high school, and the University of Maryland was 80 to 90 percent white. On top of the pressures of being in a mostly white environment, I was struggling financially. I was having a great time at the University of Maryland, but I really just needed a job at this point.

By the time I realized I needed a job, I had only two classes to take before I graduated. I realized I would not be able to go to law school immediately, but I did manage to finish my two classes and graduate from college before joining the police force.

I went to the police academy in the beginning of 1987. For me, I was just there for the money, and in the hopes that I'd help someone. In my mind, I think I rationalized that I was going to help people.

I only planned to stay a short time, but that short time became seven years. My goal was to do this for one or two years, at the most. I was then going to get out and go to law school. I worked in a really high-crime area. There were a lot of murders while I was there. One thing that is unique to our capital is that a day doesn't go by that there isn't a shooting of some kind. It wasn't uncommon to hear gunshots and it wasn't uncommon for someone to shoot at you. That was a common occurrence.

As a police officer, I felt I was different. I was this feminist cop and I was coming from this place of feminism. I felt that I was the antithesis of what an officer was supposed to be made of. While most police officers were trying to mete out justice as usual, that wasn't at the forefront of what I was all about. I was more into social justice, and that's not what cops are usually after. But I was able to find a place there also that was comfortable for me. My fellow officers treated me well. I am grateful for the other women who paved the way for me in my job. I came into police work at a time when feminism had been an issue for more than two decades.

I do think that misogyny was still extremely high, though. The difference was that I was working in the area where I grew up. It was where I went to high school, where my friends lived. Working in the same area in which I grew up, I found it difficult at first, but eventually it worked to my advantage. There were a lot of people I grew up with, especially the people in my neighborhood, who were into drugs or had addictions. In a rather odd way, these people were respectful of my position. When I was around or whenever they saw me, they would either go the other way or not put me in a position of having to arrest them.

Sometimes I would have to arrest someone I knew, but I always remembered that when I made drug-related arrests, I was keeping poison out of the community. I would think, This is someone who's poisoning people in my community. I'm keeping someone from selling this stuff to children, because my family lives here, too.

Eventually, I got a promotion to plainclothes vice officer in the drug-control unit. One night, I heard a call for shots fired, possible person down on the railroad tracks. I was the first officer there. When I got there, I jumped out of the car and went over to the railroad tracks. People were pointing to where the shooter was running along the railroad tracks. I found the victim lying on the tracks, shot through his eye.

I remember feeling really sick. I could hear the sirens coming and I had to suck it up because I didn't want anybody to see me reacting to it. What I recall is that I just stood there like it didn't bother me, but inside, I was really so bothered by it.

Homicide handled the case from there.

During my seven years on the D.C. police force, I worked mostly in vice. I was only on patrol for about eight months before I got promoted to vice.

Originally, I had been sent to vice for thirty days to observe the vice officers during drug busts. While I was there, an incident happened. I had followed the vice cops to a drug house. I had just been taking stolen-car reports, that kind of thing. I had never been involved in any kind of drug stuff in patrol.

I followed the vice team into an apartment building and down to a basement apartment, which was supposed to be an abandoned apartment. They knocked on the door and a young man answered.

They push him aside and walk past him. He was really scared. This is a drug bust. I remember we all had our guns out.

The vice squad shut the door. I had my gun in my hand. The team walked by the kid, but he was standing there with a big gun in his hand. I'm standing there with a gun in my hand and we are like looking at each other. They just walked right by him. He's eighteen, maybe seventeen. I could tell he was scared. I just reached out and grabbed the gun.

In the next room, there was another guy with a gun. They got the gun from him and then they came back to the front room and I showed them the gun I'd taken away from the kid. I told them that they'd all walked by him while he had a gun in his hand.

They were so happy. He could have shot them in the back. He was so scared. Who knows what he would have done?

The team hadn't really looked at the kid who answered the door because he looked harmless. That's a big mistake to make when working a drug bust. They moved him behind the door. He was standing behind the door, and I was the last person in. They all walked by, rushed into this back room. When I shut the door, there we were, standing there looking at each other. That was quite an experience. I knew he was really scared. It never crossed my mind to shoot him. A lot of people say why didn't you shoot him, he's standing there with a gun. It didn't cross my mind. He was like a child to me. He was clearly scared, and that was the right thing to do. I thought it was tragic also because we did find his crack cocaine. Here is this kid who is going to be in jail for twenty years.

After this incident, the vice squad told me that they were keeping me. At the time, I was the only woman in the department. There probably were women before, but at this time there were none.

As a vice officer, I got to wear plainclothes and do some undercover work. My main goal as an officer with vice was to find out who was the drug dealer or who the source was, and then gather information through confidential sources. The vice unit would target a drug dealer, send an undercover officer out to make a buy, and arrest the dealer.

Drug cases could manifest themselves in a couple of ways: One way was that the officers would ride around and gather information from people on the street. You might find out where the dealer lives and watch their house or do surveillance. Gathering information would be standard before getting a search warrant.

Another way for the officers to find out about a drug dealer would be to use a confidential source. The officers would have that source go in and make a buy from the dealer. That is a basis for a search warrant.

Sometimes officers would get an anonymous tip over the phone. That would be a source of initiating an investigation.

Most of the sources I found, or at least the best sources, the ones with the best information, in my experience, came from people who were caught themselves. These sources were trying to help the police in order to lighten their own load. Even better was getting a tip from a disgruntled partner. Usually that was the demise of many. I thought that was great.

In my experience, the television scene with the police in the interrogation room with the suspect never happened in my district. There was so much crime and so few cops on the street. You could go to work and there would be six cops on the street for the whole area. We didn't have an interrogation room. Our detectives didn't even do that. I think the experience is maybe different in other places. I think homicide would probably do that more than anybody else. In vice, you didn't have time to interrogate people.

By the time I made an arrest, I wasn't looking to get the suspect to confess. The evidence that my team and I had gathered was able to stand on its own.

The truth is, D.C. is really kind of different. I only know that from working there and from working in the Boston area now on the defense point of view.

In Boston, the police officer is the one who actually has the power to make an arrest. It's very strange here. The police have so much power here. The police actually formulate the charges. They say you are going to be charged with this, that, and the other. They can just [do that] for whatever they want. Whether it's by the legal standard is another issue. So they constantly overcharge people here.

In the District of Columbia, in Washington, D.C., for example, if you know you are charging them with drugs, basically you put down the drug offense or possession with the intent to distribute drugs. But before that actually becomes the formalized charge, the next day or the same day, if there's time, you would report to the U.S. attorney's office, because it's federal. Since D.C. is not a state. You would say, this is what happened. You would relate the events to the attorney. "This is what was recovered. This is all my evidence." They would say, this sounds like you have that, or they would say, no, it is going to be suppressed. No, we are not going to go for it with this. Yes, this is a very good case and you can add these additional charges. The attorneys would do the charges. It's really different.

One case that sticks with me had to do with the mandatory minimum. I had a search warrant for a man's apartment—well, I call the man a kid. I say "kid" because I don't think he was more than nineteen. We found about seven bags of crack and a gun. I don't think the gun even worked. The value of the crack was approximately two hundred dollars if he sold it on the street. This was one of my first drug busts. My colleagues told me to take the case to the federal court. In D.C., an officer has a choice of D.C. superior court or the federal court. This was five grams of crack, which is nothing. I said okay, I'll take it to federal court, and I did.

The young man ended up getting six to seven years. I then realized that I thought that was too harsh. That wasn't really a just result. I think that in my mind, this was a turning point for me. I felt that I was just treating the symptoms and I realized that this wasn't really how I wanted to use my time and talents.

The same amount of powder cocaine can make more crack. You can cook it into crack and make three times as much crack. So really, the powder is more, having the powder is more than having the crack, because it is already cooked and broke down. It's like the drug of choice for the poor. I didn't really understand that at the time. I wish I had understood that at the time. That is one of the things that I take with me now. I think about all these kids who had a gun that didn't work, and they had five rocks of cocaine and they are doing five to seven years in jail. If they'd had three times that in powder, they would be out in six months. It's crazy.

If the young man had had the same amount, five grams, of cocaine, he would have been subject to a year in jail as opposed to six or seven years for crack.

These young black males are being subject to these minimums, where if they had the same amount of powder cocaine, they would maybe have a year in jail and for the same amount of crack, fifty years in jail.

D.C. is pretty integrated in the police force. D.C. has a 62 percent black population. It is a primarily black force, but the midmanagement is overwhelmingly white. It has changed so much. There was always some sort of drama going on in the police department. Even after I left, I kept up with the drama.

There was always drama with Mayor Marion Barry. I remember one instance in 1986 or early '87 when the mayor went on a raid with me to a drug house. At the time, I thought we were getting a handle on crack. Barry was with us as we went into this house. It seemed funny to me. He was standing there. We found some drugs in this house and the mayor said, "That's a fifty-dollar rock." We all looked at him like, How do you know that is a fifty-dollar rock? He then said, "Ain't it?" Like he was qualifying now. He knew exactly what it was.

That was an enlightening moment. This was before his troubles and we were all wondering how he knew that it was a fifty-dollar rock. Back then, a person wouldn't know about the price of crack unless he or she used it. Most people would think, Who would pay fifty dollars for that little thing, unless this is what you do for work, or you're a chemist, or you work in a lab. How does the mayor of Washington know this is a fifty-dollar rock?

Most people weren't surprised to learn that the mayor was on drugs. They were more surprised that he got caught. I also think they spent too much money to get him. There was all this money on the investigation because people thought he was too much of a Teflon mayor, but what was true was that he was just a very nice person. He was reelected. It was a good climate in D.C. to work in, in many ways. I made more being a police officer than I do being a defense attorney, working for the Commonwealth of Massachusetts, which requires me to have a minimum of two degrees and pass a bar exam. I find that very interesting. I made much more, volumes more, financially as a police officer. So the mayor, I would say he definitely took care of the people who worked in government.

I knew that police work would have an effect on me to some extent. I told myself that when I started to see that it was really affecting my personality, my worldviews, then it was time for me to move on. I was able to see this effect on me. I think I was really in touch with what was going on with myself.

Coming from my background, I feel privileged—I made it out— yet I don't feel that I helped people when I was a police officer. I don't come away from it with a sense of pride. I feel that definitely the community needs protecting and you need police, but for me that is not how I want to use my time or talents. I feel like I need to use it to uphold people's rights.

And I don't think police work does that. You can become so desensitized that in your mind, you formulate who the criminal is.

One day I was at my house and all my friends were over. I looked at them and realized that they were all cops. I thought, I work with these people, I don't want to see them on the weekend. I felt that my friendships with my fellow workers were jeopardizing my ability to see right from wrong. It's to the point where, when someone does something wrong, you have to protect them. I think it's a dangerous thing to give somebody with a high-school diploma and six months of police training in a police academy, a badge and a gun and put them on the street. A lot of my colleagues had some great strengths in police work, but were weak in other areas because of their lack of education.

When I was in vice, because I had the most education of anybody there, I did the writing. I would proofread people's reports because a lot of my colleagues and my partner, they didn't write that well. I often used to wonder, as much as I loved him, How did you get out of high school? But he was an incredibly smart officer. His intuition, his sense of justice, and his sense of treating people fairly were really intact. And he started to write better and kept doing it.

Still, I wasn't happy as a police officer. My dream to go to law school was still there, as strong as ever.

There comes a time when you just have to quit, and that is what I did. One of the reasons I decided to leave was that I realized that I was becoming desensitized. A dead body didn't faze me. I could look at someone's brains on the ground and I could go and eat. I thought, This is not good.

I recall what my training officer told me—if you don't get out in five to seven years, you're stuck. I just made it with seven years on the force under my belt. He knew that I was different than everyone else. He didn't really discourage me, but he just knew what my vision was. He would say, "Hey your time is running out. If you don't leave, you're going be here."

I chose to go to New England Law School in Boston. I still had a house to sell and I had just bought a car. I decided I just had to do it. I had a four-hundred-dollar-a-month car payment. My house was practically new and it was remodeled, so I sold it and went to Boston. I drove the car, and I had really nice furniture and I basically gave it away. I said, "I have to get out of here. The handwriting is on the wall. I'm never going to leave if I don't leave now." I just felt like I've got to go. My family thought I was absolutely crazy.

Today I work as a public defender in the Commonwealth of Massachusetts, in Boston. I don't make the money I made as a police officer on the District of Columbia force, but I'm happier with myself.

My sister is a respiratory therapist. She was supposed to be a doctor. I held up my end of the bargain.

Officer Angela Pate

Chicago Police Department

I grew up with both of my parents and two older brothers on the southeast side of Chicago. I went to a public grammar school, then an all-girl Catholic high school.

For some strange reason, my eighth-grade teacher suggested to my mother that I go to a military academy. I said I'm staying in Chicago. I'm not going to a military school. He seemed to think that I could get good discipline in a military school. Still, I graduated. He was my eighth-grade teacher, my homeroom teacher, my science teacher. And he was the minister of my mother's church.

My teacher and minister must have been onto something, because my mother and I eventually settled on a Catholic school in the area. Looking back on it, I believe that if I had gone to a public school I might not have graduated. I never liked school from the fifth grade on. I really didn't.

Being taught mostly by nuns didn't do anything to tame my spirit. The nuns weren't wearing the habits and everything when I graduated in 1978. The old nuns still wore them, but the new ones coming through, they wore blue jeans and sweaters. It was like a hippie crowd. It was okay. It was different.

After graduation, getting into police work was happenstance for me. I wasn't sure what I wanted to do, but I did know a couple of police officers. When the test was available, I took it at the same time as my cousin did. By the time I should have found out about the test, I had moved, and a few weeks later, when I was talking to my cousin, it was suggested that I look into whether I'd passed or not.

I called the next day and was told that they'd get back to me. Two days later, on a Friday, I was getting ready for work when I got a call, telling me to report to the academy on Monday morning. I got back in my van and said, "I don't believe this." I said to myself, "Do you really want to do this?" I decided to try it. I've been there ten years, so I guess it's been pretty good.

I was first assigned to Sixty-first and Racine in the Seventh District. Seventh was an exciting district for a rookie to work in. Different districts got different calls, and oftentimes in other districts, a police officer would be called to a scene that didn't exist or that didn't require police assistance. In the Seventh District, calls that came in were real; whatever they said happened, happened.

I remember that during my first year on the force, a man's head was found in the alley and his body was discovered on the next block. Where I'm at now, they just call the police for bully tactics. "I'm going to call the police if you don't leave me alone." But over in Seventh, very seldom what they called you about wasn't true.

One of the things that I recall as a good experience was that I became a "floater" during my first few weeks on the job. Instead of having one training officer, I got to ride with several different officers, and far from being unsettled by it, I considered it a good experience. I was able to see how different officers worked, take the advice they gave me, and figure out how best to work in the things I learned from each officer.

The guy who was assigned to train me broke his hand. I never met him. To this day, I don't think I've ever seen this man. I was going from person to person, the ones they call the good officers and the ones no one wanted to work with. I worked around a lot of different people for about two weeks until I was assigned a guy who worked with me for the rest of my training.

The first case I ever broke also happened during my first few months as a rookie. I was reading the police bulletins that came out daily and noticed that some crates had been stolen off the railroad tracks.

We went over to this guy's house—I don't even know why. I think a lady called and said her boyfriend pulled a gun on her. We're looking all around. I'm nosy, for one thing. I looked in the refrigerator and freezer. I found two guns in the freezer in a plastic bag. We looked around and we found some bikes. The bikes were the same ones from off the railroad tracks.

It was all in a day's work.

The calls I hate getting the most are anything involving children. You get a thick skin, but some things you just can't shake—like kids, anything with children. You try not to take it personal, but sometimes you just can't. You look at the mother, you want to break her back. But you have to be professional. It's hard to shake it—so hard to shake it when it has to do with kids.

One of the most memorable weeks in my career as a police officer involved three cases, all of them involving children.

The first call was from a person who lived in the projects and who had observed three children living on their own for the last few days. The neighbor had called the police to let them know that she had heard water running. She had knocked on the door, but no one would answer. When I arrived, the window was open on the outside on about the fifth floor of this project. I went inside the building and heard the water running.

My fellow officers and I had to do a forced entry. We found the children living in squalor. The oldest girl was about four years old. Her little sister was two years old and the youngest was nine months old. The place was filthy. It was like roaches in the baby's Pampers.

The four-year-old autistic child was feeding her younger siblings peanut butter. She acted like she was the mama. She was trying to watch TV. She wouldn't open the door for anybody or anything.

My fellow officers and I went searching for the mother. We found her down below on a playground near the projects. She was high on crank. When we questioned her, it was clear that the children had been left alone for at least two days. The mother had needed to buy drugs and had sold the children's clothes to feed her habit.

She was just nonchalant about it. "Well, I needed some drugs and so I sold the baby's clothes." You want to go out there and say, what is your problem?

I found the children in the morning, and stayed with them all day, which may be why this is such a memorable case. You have to go to the hospital with them and then they get attached to you. I wanted to take them home with me. I took the girls to the hospital to see if they had been abused.

They needed to be washed up and the oldest girl wouldn't let anyone but me touch her. They get attached to you as the time goes on. After the visit to the hospital, I had to take the girls to a custody hospital and left them there. They went into foster care soon afterward.

In the same week, the second case came in. I went on a call about another family of children left on their own. The mother was gone, on drugs. The grandmother was on dialysis, so she had to leave the house to get her kidney treatment. The aunt lived downstairs.

She called. She was tired of her sister walking off and leaving her kids, taking advantage of their mother.

The aunt wasn't being hard-hearted; she was already taking care of two other children, one being a seven-year-old girl who was mentally challenged and who had crippling arthritis. The aunt had to bring her to and from home on the bus. The aunt also had a baby to take care of. She had just had enough.

The most haunting call of all happened in the same week. I went on a call to a house where an eleven-year-old boy had hung himself in the closet in a house full of people. There were four generations living in the house—the grandmother, the mother, the aunt, and cousins. No one but the eight-year-old brother noticed his brother hanging in the closet. Why didn't they all notice that he hung himself? It was four rooms. Why didn't they see him? It wasn't like a real closet. It was a place where you hang your clothes. There were no doors. It was like a pole with a curtain across it. There was no reason they shouldn't have seen this little boy over here—hanging off the pole in the closet.

His little brother cut him down because the adults didn't believe that his brother was in there. The child is probably scarred for life.

That one week took a lot out of me. The first thing you think of is that some people can't have kids and you all are having kids like rabbits. Why don't you just not have any, give them up for adoption or something because you aren't taking care of them? They don't have to be here. I also had an encounter with a lady named Rosemary. Rosemary had been hit on the head and, if she didn't take her medicine, she would just go off. She was violent. She had been in jail for killing a man before, years ago.

She called the police to tell them that her boyfriend was molesting her granddaughter. When my partner and I answered Rosemary's call, she told us that she had seen her boyfriend's hand under her granddaughter's blankets. She didn't know if he had done anything to her, but she had seen his hand under the blanket with her granddaughter. I took the granddaughter and Rosemary to the hospital.

I asked Rosemary, "Did you take your medicine?" She said she had. She said she was going to kill him.

My partner and I went downstairs where the boyfriend lived and we took him in and locked him up. We pulled the children aside and asked what happened. Both children told us that the boyfriend had pulled on the girl's panties.

We asked them if the boyfriend had touched her. We didn't want to scare the girl but we wanted to get at the truth.

There wasn't really anything wrong with her. They couldn't tell me if he was fondling her. He hadn't caused any damage to her.

One of the detectives knew Rosemary because he had charged her when she had committed the murder. He had called her a multiple murderer. That's how I found out she had killed someone before.

But that wasn't the end of the story. Some time went by, and I continued to work in the district. I'd get calls from time to time from Rosemary to come to her house because someone would call about her or she would call about something.

They gave me the call one day and I was working by myself and she had three or four daughters. They said, they only sent you? I said, what do you mean?

One of the daughters explained that her mother was in the house and she was real strong. Apparently Rosemary was so angry that she had broken the cast-iron range grids that held the pots above the flame. I didn't want to prove them wrong, so I sent for backup. Two male officers showed up.

When we all went up, she opened the door and she was looking like she needed some serious medication. I called her name. Rosemary's whole attitude changed and she told me that her daughters were trying to put her in the hospital. She didn't want to go.

"You went to the hospital with me last time," Rosemary told me. "They are trying to drag me out of here. I don't have any clothes. Come into the room with me so I can put on my clothes." Although I was a little leery at the prospect of being alone with Rosemary, I went with her. She had a gown on and she wanted to put on some jeans.

I told her that I would accompany her to the hospital, but Rosemary had to promise that she'd stay there and take her medicine.

I went into this room and she locked the door. I'm thinking, Please don't let her snap while I'm in here by myself. She was fine. I talked to her and she held my hand all the way out the door. I enjoy the district I work. I have characters I regularly see. And if I don't know some of their Christian names, I make one up for them. One homeless man has been named the Troll of Fifty-fifth. This has nothing to do with his outward appearance, but with his behavior. It's this guy with one leg. He's on crutches.

The first time I encountered him, he was standing in the middle of the street like a bulletin board. He wouldn't let cars through unless they gave him money. When the light changed, he would hop out and stand in front of a car. If you got out of the car and told him to move, by the time you got back in your car, he would have hopped right back out there. So we go over and make him get out of the street. I don't even know this guy's name. He just argues, curses, and hollers. What can you really do to him? We took his crutch away one day. Somebody else put him in another district for a while. He's back again.

Sometimes things can get a little bit too exciting for me. One night, my partner and I were just across the street from the next district when we got a call that shots were being fired about two blocks from where our district ended.

There were two districts on the same radio zone. We could hear their calls. There was a man down.

We decided to go there and see who was shot. It was a high-rise. My partner and I decided to drive by and see what was going on.

We went by and we see this ambulance and police car, but we don't see no body. Then we hear these shots firing out. Using my logic, what I'm thinking is, whoever shot the guy, they didn't want him to live. I figured that the shooters were firing to keep the paramedics from the body. They were shooting to keep the police from getting to the body and the man was just lying there in the street.

So now we duck down behind the car because we knew what was going on. They started shooting again, because they thought we were going to try to go to the man's body. They started shooting out the building.

My partner and I hid behind a parked car and, along with the paramedics and other police officers, waited out the shooters. We couldn't see where the shots were coming from and we felt helpless.

The police and paramedics talked about driving the wagon to the body, so they could get the body and put it in the ambulance, but there was a high risk of the driver getting shot.

People were saying things. I guess people think you're invisible because you are police. You are human like everybody else. People were saying things like, "You aren't even doing anything." My mouth is bad—I have a bad mouth. A guy I didn't even know came over and said that. I said, "You go get him. I don't want to get shot. You go drag him to the ambulance."

Another case that I remember happened when Officer Joe Davenport and I were working the wagon. I've had my share of dead bodies. The most eerie one I had, Joe Davenport and I were working together. We got off work at eleven, and we got a call at a quarter to eleven. I knew this person was dead. I just knew it. I said, someone's dead and it's almost time to go home.

We went to the call, another project building, and found that the door was unlocked. It was just like an Alfred Hitchcock movie. I could feel in my bones that there was a dead person in that apartment. It was a woman, and she was nude. All her pubic hair had been shaven off. One side of her face had been beaten in. She had been strangled with the straps of a jumper or a pair of overalls.

The call was traced, and it turned out that the man who had killed her had made the call, telling 911 that there was a disturbance in the victim's apartment. When the police questioned him later, he tried to put suspicion on the woman's boyfriend, but the boyfriend had a solid alibi for that night. The forensics team found the razor in the garbage and the police were able to trace everything back to the man who had raped her, killed her, and then notified the police about the body. He broke down and admitted his crime.

Despite, or maybe because of, the excitement, I do enjoy my work. I have worked patrol since my first day on the force ten years ago, and I enjoy the firsthand, up-close work that I do. I work in a pretty rough district. It's pretty bad. The only thing in my favor is that they don't like cold weather and they don't like the rain. If it rains or snows, it's not that bad. If it's hot out, then everyone's out.

During my ten years on the force, I feel I haven't really been in the crossfire of racial tensions. I attribute this to the fact that I get along with people and the times. I haven't had any problem with anyone. You hear people talking. If things don't go their way, they say, well they don't like me because of this or that. I haven't had that experience.

Officer Nora Smelser

Chicago Police Department

There are officers in the Chicago Police Department who have more experience than I do. There are those with more rank; with more time served on the street. And there are many officers who work as diligently at their job as I do.

But I like to think there is no cop on the Chicago force who works *harder* and *more diligently* to be a good cop than me.

I am a patrol officer presently assigned to the Second District. In addition to the same duties shared by my fellow officers, I also serve as watch secretary, which means that I am the one who does the sheets (the administrative paperwork for my watch).

Besides working as a full-time cop, I also hold two secondary jobs . . . in addition to going to school!

At the beginning of a normal working weekday, I'll show up for employment at the Chicago Board of Education, five days a week, Monday through Friday, working mornings before I report to work as a police office. I am assigned to the board's security section. My time of duty is from six A.M. until ten A.M., and my duties are numerous enough to keep me constantly active throughout my shift. These duties include making sure that the many visitors get to where they are supposed to be. The board has teachers, and other people working for the board, coming and going every day for meetings, fingerprinting, or any number of reasons. It's a busy place and, Chicago being the way it can be, there have been problems from time to time. But mostly the work is strictly routine.

In addition to helping direct people, I am also charged with routine inspections such as making sure that people who are taking office equipment out of the building are authorized to do so, et cetera. For the most part, I have found that my hours at the board go by quickly. Both jobs—being a cop and working security—suit me just fine.

I am thirty-four years old, single, and—what with a couple of side jobs and my full-time police work—I do my best to maintain some semblance of a private and a social life. But such valiant efforts often seem to be in vain.

I have chosen to dedicate my life to my job as a police officer.

Perhaps the best way to illustrate this would be not to focus on one of my typical workdays on the job, but rather to follow me through a more or less typical "day off" in the life of one hardworking policewoman.

So what do I do on a day off?

Let's skip Saturdays. I attend classes on most Saturdays.

I'm grateful that my superiors have been lenient enough to allow me to have set days off. The department has rotating days; an officer works a total of six consecutive days before being given a day off. I had wanted to take more than one class on Saturday and, because I wanted to devote time to the class and also to study after school at the library, I have been allowed to take off Saturdays and Sundays. This has helped a great deal in the pursuit of my degree in organizational management. These classes are part of an accelerated program at the University of Concordia, located in a suburb of Chicago about twenty minutes from my home in River Forest, a setup that is exactly what I had hoped to structure. And I am attending class with people close to my own adults working on a degree. I had not looked forward to the prospect of sitting in a classroom with a bunch of bored and restless eighteen-year-olds. Most importantly, pursuing my education at Concordia will facilitate obtaining a degree in the shortest amount of time. This is my next step toward finding a real career within the Chicago Police Department. I have no complaints about my present position, but I do not always want to be in patrol.

I know something about the Chicago PD's history. As a woman *and* an African-American, I'm in an ideal position to observe firsthand the state of race relations within the department today. Every day I witness and experience, and in fact my life *represents,* the realities and potential of a black officer's life in the department today. I understand that not so very long ago, there was a time when the police department was almost solely white male Irish. There is still widespread nepotism and the good-old-boy system is securely entrenched. And, Chicago being a political city, the department is likewise very political.

However, I am basically an optimistic person. With my degree, I see no reason why I cannot fulfill my career goal as a police officer. This is the reason I'm working so hard to get that degree with as little delay as possible. The way I see it, my education will then be no grounds for being turned down for positions within the department that I hope to apply for.

And so Saturday, one of my two days off, is a school day. And of course weeknights are often also spent cracking the textbooks. The remainder of a typical Saturday is generally taken up with what little time I have allowed myself for errands, chores, friendships, family, and all of the other normal realities of a person's everyday life.

And so we'll skip Saturday.

Instead, for a look in on one of my days off, let's look at one of what have been many "typical" Sundays. . . .

My second "second job" is what is termed, within the department, as "special employment." Whereas my employment as a security officer at the board of education constitutes working on my own time as an off-duty policewoman, special employment, on the other hand, concerns working in my capacity *as* a Chicago police officer, thereby as a representative of the department. However, the difference here is that I *am* working the special-employment job on my off-duty hours. In other words, if I were to be injured while working this special employment, I would be covered by medical insurance but I would be considered as having been injured *on my own time,* not on duty. It may sound tricky, and it can be. But it's the reality of special employment.

There are many officers like me who like to work special employment. On a day off, officers can make the same rate of pay as they do on their regular jobs.

I work special employment usually on the average of three Sundays per month. When working special employment, I work on the Chicago Transit Authority's city buses.

The CTA has a contract with the police department in an effort to ensure that riders on city buses, as well as CTA employees, are safe. When working the CTA, there are two different positions an officer can take: You can work plainclothes or you can work in your uniform. I have worked both. In plainclothes, the officer is on the bus waiting for someone to do something illegal, waiting for someone to smoke or drink alcohol or spray graffiti or buy or sell or use drugs. In this capacity, I make arrests all the time, but nothing that I have ever considered particularly dramatic. When I'm working in uniform, I'm essentially doing the same thing but on working proactively as a *visible* deterrent to illegal activity.

I've been working the CTA ever since successfully completing my one-year probationary period on the force, officers being required to have served for one year before being allowed to work secondary employment. I then completed my ten weeks of CTA training with a field training officer, the same FTO I'd been assigned during my first weeks on the force after I'd graduated from the police academy. Since I was accustomed to working with this FTO, when I was eligible to work secondary employment, I had asked if he would be willing to go down and work CTA with me. He was agreeable to helping show me the ropes.

Sergeant Timmons is a middle-aged black male, a veteran patrol officer; a hardworking family man who seems to love his wife and his job on the force in equal parts, to hear him tell it, a by-the-book FTO with the human touch; qualities I observed and learned from our time spent together. I still have a great deal of admiration and respect for Sergeant Timmons.

But I still remember something that happened on that first day of working special for CTA. We were working that first day from six A.M. until two P.M. At least, I had *thought* that would be my first day on the job. But I got confused about the date. I was deeply disappointed and apologetic for having gotten Sergeant Timmons up so early in the morning to go down there, despite his typically generous acceptance of my human error.

Within minutes, though, my eternal optimism surfaced when three officers didn't answer up when their names were called in that morning's roll call. Those people, scheduled for CTA, hadn't come in.

I remember whispering enthusiastically to my FTO, "Sarge, we can still work!"

Timmons got a look on his face that I couldn't read. He was usually serious of demeanor, but this was that and something else. He turned away.

"No," he said in a muted voice. "It doesn't work that way. If you're not scheduled to work, you can't work."

I filed that information away along with the many other things the sarge taught me when we did begin "working CTA" together. And I'd remembered the sarge's words of that day about a month later when I was working special employment again, without him.

Another female officer showed up. The woman was white. I heard her say to a white duty sergeant, "Hey, Sarge, I'm not supposed to work today but I didn't have anything to do so I figured I would come down."

Whereupon the duty sergeant had replied, "Okay, sure. No problem."

And just like that, the woman officer was working.

I remember asking myself, Now did he do this because she was white, or did he do this because he liked her? I didn't know. I couldn't know. It could have happened either way.

Then it happened again.

The following week, I was again working special employment. A couple of white officers were not present at the close of the day at six P.M. I hadn't really thought anything about it until a female officer I was working with said, "Oh yeah, they left early."

"They left early?"

"Yeah. They're friends of the sarge, so he let them get off early."

Here again, the same situation. Was it because these white officers were friends? Or was it racism? I wasn't sure, then or now, if in a low-keyed situation like that, a black person could ever truly know for sure. I did feel slighted. But I have managed to avoid butting heads with superiors over this sort of thing mainly because, in my on-duty police-work environment, I don't encounter much that is suggestive of racism within the department. I prefer to believe that the racial walls are coming down; that between officers on a daily basis, there is not a "we and them" kind of attitude.

When "working special," I have worked with both white and black partners.

On *this* Sunday, I was working the ten-to-six watch. My partner was a black male officer named Grier. We were in uniform.

A few things had changed since I'd started CTA. When I first began, officers were not required to wear a uniform. While all other watches were mandatory in uniform, the CTA special watch, from ten A.M. to six P.M., used to be only plainclothes. That was the main reason I had started working from ten to six. I didn't necessarily want to be in uniform on a day off. Unfortunately, a problem had developed with too many officers just showing up for work and not doing anything. It was a free day as far as they were concerned. They would go out for assignment and then not do anything. They would make no arrests. They would hardly get on the bus. They would just take the paycheck. These days, an officer is required to call in the day before, to be informed whether to show up in uniform or plainclothes.

And so this particular Sunday of special work began at ten A.M. with Officer Grier and me showing up for roll call.

Our first CTA assignment of the day was to stand on the train platform at Seventy-ninth and Western for two hours; our foot post from eleven A.M. until one P.M.

With the full array of humanity swirling about us there at the train stop, our presence was meant to be—and generally is—a deterrent to the type of crime that has unfortunately become all too common in such high-density areas, crimes ranging from purse snatching to drug dealing to rape, and more than a few face-to-face confrontations at such locations have resulted in someone being pushed into the path of a fast oncoming train.

Grier and I spent our two hours monitoring the constant flow of people boarding and departing the trains that clattered in and out of the stop. Passersby ranged from kids to the elderly, from professionals at work or play on their day off to hunkering gangstas who belligerently flashed their signs while maintaining a respectful distance from us and obeying the law at least for the time being.

Grier and I had worked as partners on this job before. We are of similar age and background. Grier didn't talk much about himself, which was okay with me. I'd heard he was a divorced dad, but I considered that none of my business. I only knew from working with him that Grier was a good cop, trustworthy and competent. We made for good partners.

After leaving the foot post, we got thirty minutes for a lunch break.

Then we worked until five thirty P.M., riding buses.

This day's assignment resulted in eighteen bus rides. That may not sound like a lot, but cumulatively it's an undertaking that involves considerable effort and travel from location to location. You have to hustle, catching eighteen bus rides, staying on each bus for five minutes, plus time spent waiting at the stops where crimes can occur similar to those at a train stop.

When a pair of officers work this assignment, one officer drives, following in a marked patrol car, while the other officer rides the bus. Grier and I liked to trade off, and spent that afternoon taking turns riding the specified five minutes (or a quarter mile) on the buses. Most officers simply time their rides with their wristwatch.

There's another step in the procedure that's changed since I began working CTA. In the past, an officer just had to get on the bus, ride, and get off, duly noting the bus number (on the outside of the bus) and the run number (which is inside the bus), along with the driver's name and badge number. These days, we are issued pass cards that are used to clock us. In the past, there had been far too many cases of people who did not ride the bus at all, or who did not ride for the full five minutes. Now it's possible to effectively track officers working CTA. But for honest, hardworking cops like Grier and me, who've been doing our job correctly all along, it's one more piece of time-consuming paperwork.

And so, fast-forward to the approach of the end of that day's special watch.

It happened at about four P.M.

I had just gotten off a bus. Grier and I were driving to our next location, through a residential, blue-collar, culturally diverse neighborhood, primarily black and Hispanic.

Grier was at the wheel. I was making some notations in my report book, and so did not see the accident.

Grier said, "Heads-up."

I snapped shut the notebook and glanced up as he switched on the blinker lights. We slid through an intersection. I saw the fender bender then, down the street at midblock. Grier hadn't switched on the siren, and in these first few seconds after the minor accident, its participants were obviously unaware of a police car in the vicinity, coming in their direction.

A two-door sedan had bumped into another car that had been pulling out from a parking space.

The immediate reaction on the scene was that a woman driver, who had been pulling out of the parking space, panicked, becoming highly agitated. An extremely overweight, very upset late-middle-aged Hispanic, she was screaming in Spanish, appearing terribly frightened, frantically rolling up her windows, locking her car doors.

This only served to encourage the occupants of the other car. Rather than apologize or seek to calm the upset woman, three young black men were taunting her with sneering verbal abuse and gang signs. They ceased this behavior immediately upon realizing that a police car with flashing lights was coasting to a stop directly behind them.

At that point, their vehicle, a rusting two-door sedan of indeterminate age, burned rubber getting away from there, speeding off down the residential street, leaving behind a lingering cloud of acrid white smoke.

I glanced at the woman, about to get out and check on her. But the lady was regaining her composure from within the locked confines of her car. She'd seen what was happening. She was motioning to the officers that she was all right.

I turned to Grier. "Let's get 'em," I said.

Grier already had the cruiser in gear. He switched on the siren and we gave chase. The other car hadn't even reached the next intersection. It was nothing to catch up with it. Grier poured on enough speed to pull past and curb them.

I only had time for a quick look at three teenage faces in that other car as Grier sped past. I saw gang colors, and expressions in that instant of escalating intensity caught midway between arrogance and anxiety. I saw no sign of weapons. Not yet, anyway. That was good.

All of a sudden, everything had escalated. There was no way of knowing what was up here. These guys could have just killed someone.

Before the patrol car had come to a complete stop, Grier and I were exiting with our weapons drawn.

The other vehicle had already stopped several feet away to avoid another collision, this one with the police car. Both of the guys from the back were starting to clamber from the backseat, shouting things to each other like, *"Go, motherfucker. Go go go!"*

I looked around and saw that the driver was already halfway across the street, running as fast as he could to get away. I assumed a two-handed shooter's stance, drew a bead, and shouted, *"Freeze!"*

The banger froze.

With traffic coming to a stop all around him, he raised his hands. He must have heard *something* in my tone.

Grier was closing in on the car, his weapon drawn, commanding the other two guys, who were now hesitating, "Get out of the car! Get out of the car *now*!"

They, too, obeyed.

Within moments, the situation was secured, and everything had *de*escalated. All three guys were handcuffed and on the ground. I covered them while Grier searched their car.

No one had been murdered. It was small-time stuff. There was the smell of marijuana in the vehicle. The car was registered to one of the guys who had been riding in the back. The driver didn't have a driver's license. That sort of thing. And these mental giants had thought that was worth making a run for it, that they could outrun a cop car on a city street.

It was a relief to me. No one wants to die, and no good cop *wants* to kill. But the truth is that when most cops are injured or killed in the line of duty, it's during domestic-violence calls or traffic stops. These bangers could have had weapons. They could have opened fire just that fast. And so yes, there was a relief. This traffic stop had been more or less routine.

That traffic stop and its aftermath, the arrest and booking the three guys, consumed what remained of that Sunday's special watch for Officer Grier and me.

For me, the next stop would be home, a long shower, a hastily prepared meal, setting out my security and police uniforms for Monday morning, and hoping that I could stay awake long enough to review notes I'd taken at the school library yesterday for one of my classes.

It was the end of a "typical day off" in the life of one policewoman.

Officer Eddie Garre

Chicago Police Department

I have been on the Chicago police force for twelve years. I served eight of those years in plainclothes, working on drug cases, going on drug raids, and even going undercover in the schools. I am now a field training officer, and one thing I believe is that cops need a little something extra. Call it an edge. In some cases, it's what keeps us alive.

I knew this cop named Bob. He had that edge. He was big, he was strong, and he was tough. Sometimes he could get a little rough with his suspects. He'd use his hands on them, and drug dealers started to complain on him. The complaints got to be pretty frequent, and the chief had a talk with Bob. He told him that he couldn't do this, he couldn't do that. Bob finally got tired of getting called in, so he asked for a foot post. He said he'd just do his job and not hurt anyone.

That was all well and good. There were no more complaints, but in his new post, Bob lost his edge. And that made him careless.

He arrested a guy, and he had him bent over the car hood while he was cuffing him. Somehow the guy twisted away and disarmed Bob. Then he killed him with his own pistol. It never would've happened if Bob hadn't lost his edge. That's what got him killed.

I don't recommend manhandling suspects as the way to get and maintain the necessary edge. My own method is more constructive.

I'm a martial-arts expert and practice jujitsu, hapkido, and other forms.

You use that stuff more than you might expect. I also teach classes in the martial arts to people who want a little bit of an edge of their own. Or in other words, to people who don't want to wind up like Bob.

Besides an edge, there are a couple of other things that I believe can help an officer: luck and a sense of humor. Most cases are solved by good police work—the patient, painstaking process of analyzing clues, interviewing suspects, and following leads. The trouble is that sometimes there are no clues, no suspects, and no leads.

But that doesn't always mean the cases don't get solved. Sometimes you get lucky. Take the case of a young man named Roy and his wife, Alicia. That was a pretty gruesome one.

Roy was, to all appearances, a bright young man just getting started in his own business. Things seemed to be going quite well for him until he came home from work one night, only to find four men with guns waiting for him in his backyard.

The men forced him into his house at knife- and gunpoint. They found his wife, Alicia, in the house, and they tied her up, too. Then they started asking them where the drugs and money were hidden.

Roy and Alicia both told the men that there were no drugs and money in the place, but the men didn't believe them. So they started sticking Alicia with their knives.

Maybe they thought that the woman would be the weakest link, or maybe they were trying to break down her husband. But their strategy didn't work. Alicia continued to insist that there was no money in the house, and there were certainly no drugs. It didn't matter what she said, however, or how often she said it. The men didn't believe her.

After persistent torturing, Alicia finally did admit that she had fifty dollars hidden in the house, but that was all. Badly cut and bleeding, she refused to change her story. The men then put the knives to work on Roy, who told them pretty much the same thing that Alicia had.

The men didn't believe him, either; but faced with two genuinely stubborn people who refused to tell them what they wanted to know, the men began tearing the house apart. In the process, they eventually found two kilos of cocaine. Convinced by their find that there were more drugs and lots of money hidden in the house, they returned to torture Roy and Alicia until they got the answer they wanted.

When they got back to the room where they had them tied up, Roy had somehow gotten out of the ropes. He shoved the men away from him, and he and Alicia made a run for it. Alicia got outside and started calling for help, but the men shot Roy in the back and killed him before he could leave the house. They didn't kill Alicia. They took the cocaine and got out of there.

When my partner and I arrived on the scene, Roy was lying dead in his own doorway, but there were no clues, no suspects, and no leads. And to make things even more difficult, there was a wife who neglected to mention the cocaine until much, much later.

Why had the men picked Roy's house? No one who knew Roy seemed to have any idea. We thought it was a case of mistaken identity. We figured that the men just had the wrong house. At first, Alicia didn't tell us that the men who killed her husband had found the cocaine. Maybe she thought that she was protecting her husband's reputation by keeping the drugs a secret, or maybe she thought that she could somehow be held responsible for their presence in the house. At any rate, she kept her secret for quite a while.

When I finally learned about the drugs, I changed the focus of my investigation. I eventually learned that Roy had formerly been a big-time drug dealer who had gone into a straight business, supposedly leaving his past behind.

Maybe he had, but his past was what got him killed.

Someone who apparently believed that Roy was still dealing had most likely set him up. But there was no way of knowing who the setup man might have been, and I didn't think the case would ever be solved.

It was, however. Over a year later, Alicia was at a party and happened to see the men who'd tortured her and killed her husband. In an even more unusual coincidence, she was with a friend who knew me and had my beeper number.

The friend called me, and the men were arrested. So far, three have been convicted of their crime. The trial of the fourth is coming up soon. But without a lot of luck, all four men would still be free.

In another instance, I figure that I got lucky three times. We were going on a drug raid. We'd already been told by an informant that the house where we were going had a fortified door. We knew there was no way we could break it down. Or, if we could, the guy we were after would have plenty of time to hide his drugs by the time we ever got inside.

How could we get inside the house before our suspect knew what was happening? We decided to create a diversion by having my partner, Steve, throw a rock through a window. When the dealer came outside to see what was happening, we would enter the house. Steve got a huge rock and heaved it as hard as he could toward the house.

And missed the window.

We were all laughing at him. And we were razzing him a little, too. So he picked up the rock and tried again.

The rock was bulky, heavy, and hard to throw. Steve missed the window a second time. We were all laughing and carrying on so much by then that the dealer must've thought some really rowdy guys had come to make a buy. He came to the door to see what was going on. Surprised, we thanked him politely for his hospitality and went inside.

That place was really a filthy mess. Dirty clothes thrown around everywhere, dirty dishes all around, dirty floors, dirty everything. But because there were no drugs in sight, we had to search for them.

We looked everywhere: in the closets, under the beds, behind the furniture.

Considering the conditions, I didn't much like putting my hand under the beds, but I had to do it. I stuck my hand under one of the beds and felt something sticky. I jerked my hand back out, and there was roach tape sticking to it. You know what roach tape is? It's that sticky paper that roaches crawl over, and they get stuck to it. That's what it was, and there were little roaches all over it, twitching around and kicking their legs.

I flicked my hand reflexively and the tape flew across room, hitting Steve, my partner, who was searching a closet.

He was wearing his vest. So he didn't feel it hit him. I walked over to him and said, "Hey, Steve, what's that on your vest?" He looked down at all those roaches kicking around, and he let out a scream.

The other officers stormed into the room with their guns drawn. They all thought Steve had been shot, and before long, everyone was laughing at Steve again.

How do I figure I was lucky three times?

For one thing, we got inside the house without even having to break a window or deal with the fortified door.

For another thing, the officers who responded to Steve's scream didn't shoot anyone.

And finally, Steve didn't shoot me.

One thing about luck, however: It balances out. Sometimes, the crooks get lucky, too. Once an outside unit came into my district to serve a warrant and requested assistance from my own unit. We went to this big apartment building, probably about thirty-four stories. The guy we were after was located up on the ninth floor. When we got to the place, we told the super not to announce us, and we went on up to the suspect's apartment.

When we arrived at the apartment door, we heard noises inside, the sounds of a television set and of someone moving around.

We knew there was someone in there. We could hear him. But nobody answered our knock. We finally had to force entry.

To our surprise, we found no one in the apartment. Even a diligent search failed to turn up anyone. There was no one in any of the rooms, no one in the closets, no one hiding under the beds or behind the couch. But there were plenty of signs that someone had been there, and the TV set was still turned on.

We were all looking at each other and saying, "What is this guy? A magician? Did he just disappear into thin air?" We figured that had to be it, because we knew somebody was in there when we knocked, and now he was gone.

At about the time we were ready to conclude that our suspect had indeed simply vanished, I heard screams from outside the apartment. I went to the window and looked out. There was a man nine stories below, lying on the ground and screaming in pain.

It was our suspect. When he heard us at the door, he climbed out the window and hung from the ledge. He was doing okay until a man in the eighth-floor apartment looked out and saw him. The guy on eight thought our guy must be a burglar, so he went and got his pistol. He told our guy that if he didn't get away from there, he was going to shoot him.

Faced with the choice of being shot or letting go, the suspect let go and fell nine stories to the ground.

What was so lucky about that?

The guy was hardly even hurt. He fell nine stories, and all he got was a broken leg and a broken hip.

Of course he also got arrested, so maybe the cops were the ones who really got lucky that time, too. There's an old line about how being lucky is better than being good. Most officers would prefer to be good, of course, but we'll take all the luck we can get.

Aaron Hol

Chicago Police Department

For the past six years, I have worked in the organized crime division in the narcotics unit. Forty years old, I have a passion for working out with weights and summertime activities like softball and bike riding. Born in Mississippi and raised in the South, I've lived in Chicago since my navy discharge twenty years ago.

This is what went down one hot summer morning on the mean streets of the West Side of Chicago.

My team had formulated a plan to make a drug buy.

The primary method of tracing illicit-drug sources is initiated at the street level through direct drug buys. The narcotics unit gets hundreds of narcotics complaints from citizens all around the city, and will regularly go out where those complaints are coming from to conduct drug stings.

On this day, my team was traveling in four separate vehicles. I was at the wheel of a Ford Cherokee, heading toward the area of Holman and Thomas.

Officer Stacy Richter rode in the passenger seat beside me. Like me, she wore dressed-down plainclothes. Stacy was Caucasian, in her late twenties; an attractive blonde.

I was trying to ignore a vague sense of nerves gnawing at my gut, and I knew why I felt that way. I was used to riding by myself.

I wheeled the Cherokee onto Holman, glancing into my rearview mirror to make sure that Meadows, another black officer, was holding his position. Dean Meadows was my second surveillance officer on this day, and he was in position, driving a rusted-out, beat-up Honda Accord, tailing from about a half block behind.

It could have been worse. I could have been out here completely alone except for this white lady riding at my side.

This stretch of Holman was lined with shabby tenement buildings and some private residences. The neighborhood had hit bottom long ago.

Vehicular and pedestrian traffic was moderate but steady beneath a baking summer sun. Jalopies and low riders passed Saabs and the occasional Porsche. This was a black neighborhood. Kids played noisily around an unloosed fire hydrant's water spray. Older folks sat on front stoops, visiting, observing the passing scene, trying to stay in the shade. Young men in gang colors strutted their machismo up and down the sidewalks while clusters of gaudy, scantily clad hookers plied their trade on street corners.

I held the Cherokee at a moderate speed. Stacy and I both eyed the passing street scene.

Yes, I understood the basis for my vague feeling of nerves. This white female officer riding beside me was my primary surveillance officer. Stacy seemed to be a nice enough young woman, with a no-nonsense professional bearing. But she was new to *this* job. And this was one job that could too easily get a man killed. Before this hour was over, my life could well depend on Officer Stacy Richter, and the plain fact of the matter was that I wasn't quite sure how she would react in a crisis.

We'd been riding in silence for ten minutes when she cleared her throat.

"Uh, is it something I said?"

I realized how preoccupied I'd been with my thoughts. "Sorry. I didn't mean to be rude."

"I know what it is." She spoke matter-of-factly, as if reading my mind. "It's that I'm new on the job. Right?" She didn't take her eyes from the passing street scene. "Don't worry. I won't let you down." Then she did glance sideways to study my reaction. "Uh, not to change the subject, but except for one of those hookers on that last street corner, I'm the only white woman I've seen so far in this neighborhood. Is that going to be a problem?"

"No," I assured her. "Plenty of players in this 'hood have white girlfriends. There are even female Caucs who drive in from somewhere else to buy drugs. As far as you being white . . . well, if anything, that counts in your favor as far as I'm concerned."

"What do you mean?"

"I mean the way you're putting your backside on the line out here on the street with me and Meadows."

She frowned. "I'm sorry. I still don't understand."

This time it was my turn to clear my throat. What the hell, I decided.

"You're new to Narcotics [unit]," I said, "but you must have noticed one thing."

She nodded. "I'm not only the token woman out here today. I'm also the only token white. Is that what you're saying?"

"That's what I'm saying."

"I did notice, of course. Ninety-nine percent of the buy officers in the buy unit are black."

"When I was in patrol," I said, "looking at the narcotics unit, I thought everyone who went into the unit would get to do all of the things that undercover police officers do. I thought everyone was working undercover, like we are."

She returned her attention to the street. "I see. But instead you found what I found. The drug buys are done by black officers. The white officers wait until the black officer has made the undercover drug buy and informs the white officers, who then close in and make the arrest. The black police officer obviously has the more dangerous position."

I was impressed. I added, "When you're undercover, you don't wear a bulletproof vest. Most buy officers don't carry a weapon. And most times you're out there by yourself. You have your surveillance officers who are watching you, but you're dealing with gang people on the street, and that's the most dangerous part of the situation." I decided to speak even more plainly. If my life could be in this woman's hands, why shouldn't I tell her the truth? "Most of the white guys don't want to do it," I said bluntly. "They want to stay back in their police cars with their shotguns and their vests on, waiting for us to make the action so they can make the arrest. I've seen it happen every day. When a black officer comes to the narcotics unit, he's immediately labeled a buy officer."

"So how do they rationalize it? That these guys we're busting *are* black?"

"The *sellers* are black," I conceded. "But there are plenty of white buyers—suburban whites coming into the city, buying heroin, buying cocaine."

"So those white cops *could* buy drugs also."

"Exactly. But most of them don't want to because they're afraid. It's too dangerous. They don't want to be on the front line. It's too risky. They don't see why they should have to risk their lives for a small amount of crack cocaine or whatever."

There was a moment of silence between us.

Then she said, "Look, I know this is dangerous work. I just want you to know that I think you're a brave man, putting it on the line the way you are."

It was a naïve thing to say. I didn't know how to respond, so I said nothing. I kept my eyes on the street.

"Over there," I said.

I'd spotted a guy making a deal at the end of a fence adjoining an alley that bisected a row of run-down dwellings. It was a block where barren front yards sparkled with shards of countless discarded crack vials.

The guy by the alley was handing over something with one hand and taking cash in return with the other from a scraggly-looking black female who could have been wearing a flashing neon sign that read JUNKIE. The woman tottered away with that listless shuffle of the drug-induced living dead, and the dealer went back to leaning idly against the fence, waiting for his next customer.

I drove past and glided the Cherokee to the curb a short distance away. Another quick glance in my rearview showed Meadows taking a parking space on the opposite side of the street beyond an intersection, seemingly wholly unrelated to what was happening here, yet affording the second surveillance officer with a clear line of vision of what was about to go down here . . . whatever that might be.

I leaned across Stacy and snapped open the glove box. I withdrew a .38 Special five-shot revolver. I leaned forward slightly, enough to slide the pistol into the waistline of my trousers at the small of my back.

Stacy observed this with open curiosity. "I thought buy officers don't carry guns."

"I don't know how brave I am," I said, opening the car door to exit, "but I'm no fool."

"I won't let you down," she repeated earnestly.

Again I didn't respond. But I did think, Girl, I sure as hell hope so!

Stacy would have the best observation of the guy he was buying from, and the best view of him. She would be relating what she saw back to the sergeant and the rest of the team, letting them know what I was doing, describing the unfolding scene to the enforcement team who were presently cruising the streets in a three-block-radius holding pattern.

Buy areas like this one always had lookouts on practically every corner. The dealers had their own enforcement unit. There were lookouts on bicycles. Sometimes there were lookouts in cars, driving around, trying to spot the team's enforcement cars. Although the enforcement team traveled in unmarked cars, they were impossible to miss in neighborhoods like this: big Chevies that everyone in town knew were police cars, manned by at least two white guys per car, all gunned up and vested.

I quelled the vague feeling of nerves stirring in my gut. Stacy would do all right, I told myself. She'd do fine. She had a quick, inquisitive mind and she'd had good training. I told myself that I had other things to focus on.

So okay, I told myself. Let's find out.

I ambled across the sun-splashed street to make the buy.

Working a drug sting calls for convincing role-playing. The rules are simple and survival depends on adhering to them. Be unobtrusive. Watch the suspect's hands as you approach. Watch for a weapon.

I sauntered up to the guy, a scar-faced, full-of-attitude nineteen-year-old in gangbanger clothes and colors. Leaning against the fence, the dealer eyed my approach with a mixture of wariness and insolence.

The game was played by getting right down to it, and so I slipped into the terminology of the street.

"You working?" I asked brusquely. *Are you selling drugs today?*

Normally you don't ask for a particular kind of drug unless they ask you.

The banger shrugged. "Yeah, I'm straight." *Sure, I'm open for business.* Also implied: *What do you want—rock [cocaine] or blow [heroin]?*

"So give me a couple," I said, as if ordering in a fast food restaurant.

The banger stepped away from the fence. He was still scrutinizing me from head to toe.

"Hold your hands up. Let me search you."

I had no choice but to raise my arms. I'd been searched before on a few occasions and already knew what I would say if the guy found the pistol. Still, things were already starting to go bad. I had hoped that this would not happen.

The banger moved forward and skillfully patted me down, and of course immediately found the .38. He not only felt the pistol stashed at the small of my back, but he started to take it out. I placed a hand on top of the guy's hand before the banger could remove the gun from its hiding place.

"Hey, man," I said, "I'm not trying to mess with anybody. The piece is for my own protection." I spoke in a reasonable tone. "I've been robbed before."

The banger jerked his hand free, leaving the gun where it was. He called out over my left shoulder, "Hey! This nigger's got a gat in his back!"

I cautiously turned to see who the guy was talking to.

Another banger—this one a spindly, pint-sized little dude, also no more than nineteen, also wearing gangsta garb and colors—was advancing rapidly along the fence. He held a 9-mm automatic, cocked, and from the distance of only a few yards away and closing, the 9-mm pistol was aimed at a point directly between my eyes.

Terror—there was no other word for it—coursed through me, but I kept the surge of emotion from revealing itself. Training and time on the street had taught me that if the terror remains, there is no escape. You can drop to your knees, beg, plead for your life. That's the best way to get killed. And so the terror did surge through me, and I quelled it. I maintained my composure, observing the gunman's approach.

This banger was nervously chewing his lower lip, obviously jacked out of his skull on something. He didn't lower the pistol as he came closer. He was muttering to himself nonstop. "Motherfucker, motherfucker, I oughta—"

He was now less than ten feet away.

Looking into the muzzle of that gun, my mind was racing. Oh my God, am I going to get shot out here? Well, if he is going to shoot, he's going to have to shoot me through my hand.

I raised a hand in a stopping gesture when the guy was practically on top of me.

"Hold it, man. I'm just here to shop. I'm a *customer*. I just came here to buy. I ain't trying to mess with nobody."

This brought two responses. The dealer's enforcer stopped muttering to himself, and he brought the 9-mm down a little. I took this as a hopeful sign. The gunman reached behind my waist and relieved me of the .38.

And that seemed to be that.

Neither guy directed words or seemingly any more attention toward me. They simply swung their backs on me and stalked off away from me, toward the alley.

I heard myself emit an audible sigh of relief. I started to turn back toward where I'd left Stacy in the Cherokee.

That's when the wired banger with the 9-mm seemed to change whatever was left of his fried mind. From about twenty feet away, both guys had paused at the mouth of the alley. The gunman whirled, tracking up one of the pistols.

"Motherfucking cop. Take this, motherfucker!"

He fired. The gunshot popped loudly, echoing from the walls of the alley.

I threw myself flat to the ground, hearing the biting snap of the round whistle close over my head, sounding almost as loud as the gunshot itself. I glanced around, looking for a spot that would provide some cover.

But both of the bangers had taken off running down the alley.

Echoes of the gunshot had faded, replaced by their laughter and running footfalls.

I was up, moving rapidly back to where Stacy and the vehicle should have been. But I drew up short before I'd gone two feet.

The surveillance car was gone!

Stacy had moved!

I bit back a curse of frustration. My intent had been to rearm, call in the enforcement team, and pursue the defendants.

Meadows' battered Accord shuddered to a stop nearby. My second surveillance officer bounded from his car as if he'd been catapulted. Meadows was heavyset, but he could move with surprising agility. He tossed me a spare revolver without slowing.

We advanced rapidly through the alley, each officer ready with his weapon in a two-handed grip, each hugging an opposite wall so as to minimize ourselves as targets.

"Why do I feel like the cavalry to the rescue?" Meadows muttered.

"Because you are," I said.

The two of us had worked the street together plenty of times before, and there was mutual respect between us.

Meadows asked, "Where's Stacy?"

"I'm wondering about that myself."

I no longer had a case of nerves. I felt no conscious fear. There was only the pumping of adrenaline raging through my system now as we moved through the alley in hot pursuit.

When we reached the far end of the alley, what I saw made relief course through me just as the terror had earlier, and I could feel my face break out in an ear-to-ear grin.

"There's Stacy," I said needlessly.

The Cherokee was angled with one front tire up on the curb, the driver-side door yawning open.

A few feet away, the wiry pint-sized gunman was facedown on the sidewalk, wrists cuffed behind his back. He'd been relieved of the two weapons. My .38 and the 9-mm were nearby on the sidewalk.

Stacy stood leaning over the guy with one foot placed securely between his shoulder blades, effectively pinning him to the sidewalk. The muzzle of her service revolver was held to the back of his head. The guy was sputtering "motherfucker this" and "motherfucker that" into the pavement.

A cluster of grade-school kids were looking on with passive interest. This was something they'd already seen in this neighborhood a thousand times before. There were witnesses on porches and elsewhere, gazing on with idle interest, but no one was leaving their shade for a closer look.

There was no sign of the first guy, the dealer I had initially approached.

Meadows and I remained separated. We approached Stacy, our pistols held up for quick target acquisition, our eyes scanning the street and buildings.

Stacy indicated a tenement across the street. "He took off through there. At the rate he was moving, I'd say he's in the Loop by now. I radioed enforcement."

This was a secondary street with practically no traffic, but suddenly, from both ends of the block, the street seemed to fill with the pair of big Chevies that came shrieking forward, sirens wailing, attachable rooftop lights flashing. The unmarked cars screeched to a halt, disgorging grim-faced white guys with badges, shotguns, and bulletproof vests.

As Stacy stepped aside, I grabbed the shooter by the scruff of his neck and yanked him to his feet. Meadows was retrieving the dropped weapons.

Then we were engulfed by the enforcement team.

I had only one second to catch Stacy's eye. I said, "Thanks, partner."

My primary surveillance officer replied with a smile, "I told you I wouldn't let you down."

Officer Stacy Richter is still in the narcotics unit, and remains one of the *few* Caucasian officers who is consistently on buy patrol.

And she does a very good job of it. Stacy has repeatedly proven herself since that first day on those mean streets.

And yet the fact remains that of all the buy officers in the narcotics unit, at this time approximately 95 percent are black. . . .

Sergeant II Wayne Guillary

Los Angeles Police Department

I grew up during the stirrings of the Civil Rights Movement of the 1960s. I was born and raised in Los Angeles, in Watts, an inner-city hotbed of turmoil and racism. Today, Watts is known by another name, South Central Los Angeles. Despite growing up in a community rife with poverty, violence, gangs, drugs, and a lack of educational funds, I came from a strong family background. Our mother, Edna, a transplanted Texan who had help in raising her three boys from her parents, raised me and my two brothers, one who is my twin. My grandfather was my inspiration and role model—he kept me and his brothers focused on positive actions throughout our youth, and steered the three of us away from bad influences. My mother worked for Douglas Aircraft, and went to school at night to try to make her life better for herself and her family.

It was while I was still living in Watts in 1965 that I witnessed my first civil unrest: the Watts riot. Although I was getting ready to turn ten at the time, the riot of 1965 left an indelible mark on my mind. A few years later, I was attending Markham Junior High School when I was involved in a gang attack. I was jumped by three guys and got stabbed. I was just a kid trying to survive, but we were all different. My older brother, Reggie, was an academian. My twin brother and I, we were just average kids who just wanted to learn something, but we also wanted to get out and have fun. My brothers and I were a little different from the other kids—thanks to our mother and grandparents, we didn't talk slang. We were taught how to use the King's English the correct way, and be proper in the enunciation of our words. So, many of the kids thought we were trying to be different and we had a tough time trying to survive.

I was supposed to attend Jordan High School in the Watts area, but by 1971, I wound up attending Los Angeles High School across town on the west side of town. To get from Watts to the west side, I had to catch three buses.

By the 1970s, gang activity had erupted on the west side: they called themselves the Crips. There were also a few local gangs, the Grims, the Pygmies, and a few others. Headlines were made when the Crips, following a concert at the Hollywood Palladium, killed a young man in Hollywood in 1971. The next day, the headlines read that the Crips had killed the son of a prominent attorney. From that point on, I can remember seeing gang members with their funny-looking hats, brims, ace deuceys, and studded diamond rocks all around their hats and earrings in their ears. It really was a very intimidating look.

In the 1970s, people thought that gangs were just small groups, but years later, gangs became established in every city, impacting Los Angeles and other cities in ways that people could never imagine, through the sale of drugs and illicit contraband, turning young children away from the family values that were once so strong. These were the issues that concerned me as I was growing up and into my adult years.

By 1965, I had witnessed some of the things that had happened to African-American people then. Of course, we were known as Negroes, but the movement was coming along to be black. James Brown and his song "I'm Black and I'm Proud" guided us into having some type of self-awareness, to be proud of who we were.

Witnessing Martin Luther King Jr. and what he was trying to do with civil rights also had an impact on me. Having witnessed the riots, I asked my mother why there was so much turmoil in the streets. My mother went on to explain that the LAPD had, in many ways, disrespected black people and that they had intruded on their personal rights to privacy. The police were violating the rights of people. I said, well, this can't be, they're the police. And my mother said, yes, but look who's policing our city, and they aren't people who look like you and me.

At that time, I vowed that I would become a policeman and change things from the inside. I first became personally aware of racial prejudice in 1968 during the Watts Festival, which was held every summer. There were policemen and sheriff's deputies patrolling the inside of the park and the perimeters to keep order.

I went over to the park for the festival one day, with a white boy. His grandparents were the only white people left in the area, and he would come visit them every summer. All of us looked forward to seeing Thomas Welch every summer. We really didn't focus on "he's white, I'm black." A Los Angeles County sheriff saw the two of us walking together and stopped us. He ordered us to come over to him.

We walked over toward the sheriff's deputies. They had on these big gold helmets with chin straps, and they were taller and bigger than we were. We were maybe thirteen or fourteen years old.

The deputy looked at the white boy and told him to move on. Not understanding the instruction, I moved on with my friend, but the deputy grabbed me before I could get very far.

The deputy asked me where I lived.

I pointed across the street. "Over there." I only lived a block from the park.

The sheriff's deputy slapped me in the face and said, "Once again, where do you live, stupid?"

I pointed across the street again.

The deputy asked a third time, "Where do you live?"

Once again I pointed and he slapped me again. I broke down and really started crying. A neighbor witnessed part of the incident and spoke up for me. "What are you doing that to him for?"

The next thing you know, there's a whole bunch of people gathering, and they called in extra reinforcements.

The deputy finally took me home. Here I got this welt slap across my face, the imprint of that deputy's hand, and the deputy was telling my mother a lie. The deputy told her that I appeared to be involved in some criminal activity in the park. My mother knew this not to be true because of who I was as a son and as an individual. They really exacerbated the situation with the lie. Here I was, looking at a public official, standing in his uniform, telling a lie.

That incident was my firsthand taste of knowing the difference between black people and white people.

At the time, my white friend and I didn't look at it as racism. All we wanted to know was why the police slapped me. I kept saying, "Why did they do that to me, Mama? Why did they do that to me?" My mother, my grandfather, and everybody was so upset by what had happened. I remember hearing the gathering crowd call out names to the sheriff's men: crackers; rednecks; KKK.

And I said, "Wow. Redneck. Cracker." And all I remember was people saying, "We're getting tired of this shit."

In 1970, there was a miniriot with the Black Panthers. I was coming into awareness, becoming cognizant of what I was as an African-American growing up in the sixties. Two years earlier, I had joined the Police Explorer Scouts, and I could see that most of the police officers were white.

I still had run-ins with officers about being black. I lived five miles from the Seventy-seventh Division where I volunteered, so I would ride my bicycle to the station. So here I am: I've got my little uniform on. I'm riding over to the station. I get to the back of the parking lot. I've been in the station for quite some time, and felt that everybody should know me by now. These two white officers stop me on my bicycle, in my Explorer Scout uniform, and they asked me, "Where'd you get this bike from?"

I thought they were joking with me at first. "This is mine. My mother bought it for me," I replied.

They said, "It's too clean. Where'd you steal it from?"

I told them I hadn't stolen it. I repeated that my mother bought it for me. I'm laughing, you know, I'm not catching on to this.

But the officers were serious. I'm thinking they're just trying to be friendly with me, till one guy says, "Get off the bike." I got off the bike and the officer looked for the serial number on the brake rod, which is at the rear of the wheel.

I reassured the officers that my bike wasn't stolen property, and that it was registered with the police department. It even had my little registered seal on it.

The officer told me to get out of there. So I go in the station. I had seen other instances where white officers would have inmates sitting on the bench, not being seen by these officers. I could be behind a partition or down a hallway and I would hear an officer say to another officer, "Hey, where's that guy at? He has the niggers down at the other end of the bench."

I was still confused by what I was party to and what had witnessed at the station, and I would bring home stories of what happened down at the station. My mother was concerned because she considered the LAPD to be nothing but a bunch of racists. And I'm saying, "God, Mama, everybody can't be racist."

As I moved on to high school, I remained an Explorer Scout and I still witnessed racists acts in the department, but I was determined to help change the department's attitude.

By the time I graduated in 1974, I had decided to join as a police student worker. You were being paid salary, but you had to go to school and you had to maintain at least a C grade average in college. So I'm going to school, I'm maintaining a C grade average, and my first assignment is in the bunko-forgery division.

My duties included making sure two barrels were filled with water every morning for coffee and to make the coffee. There were three black detectives in that division at the time. One of them came up to me and asked why I was making the coffee—the other student worker, who had been white, had been with the program for two years, and he hadn't made coffee the entire time he'd been there.

I didn't challenge his supervisor about making coffee as part of my duties, giving the lieutenant the benefit of the doubt—after all, it could have happened that the lieutenant had decided to make coffee-making part of the student worker's duties. It might have been a coincidence that the next student worker happened to be African-American. Still, I noticed that white student workers were treated differently from black student workers. They got to do things that black student workers couldn't do. We were more scrutinized—a white student worker could go out all day long, driving one of the department cars, and come back with no repercussions. A black student worker who did the same thing would end up having documents written up on him.

I didn't get into the police academy the first time I tried in 1977. There were about ninety people in that class and only five of them were black. By the time the class graduated, only one black man made it, a man named Jay Collins. I came back four years later and joined the police department in 1981. I graduated in 1982 and began working the Hollywood division.

I got assigned partners and was working with one guy whom I respected.

I really liked this guy because he was training me on how to be a good police officer and we were doing a good job. He was showing me things; he was training me.

One night on morning watch, around five in the morning, I observed a black male running down the sidewalk. I'm paying it no attention. I see this guy's got a bag in his hand, looks like a lunch bag.

I see a bus, I see this guy running, so it's obvious to me that this man is trying to run for the bus stop.

My partner suddenly said, "Where is this nigger running to?"

That just burst my bubble of what my perception of him was. Because this guy was a decent guy. He treats people right. I had worked with some white partners who wouldn't talk in the car. They'd go the whole night, maybe twenty-five words spoken to me.

There was one night when I was teamed up with another black detective, which was usually not done. His name was Billy Heard, and it was the first chance I had to work with another black detective. I think they messed up on the roll, 'cause my name's Guillary, and they said, "Well, this has gotta be a white guy."

Detective Billy Heard was considered smooth and cool, and was obviously delighted that the roll had put two soul brothers together. It was also the last time I got a chance to work with Detective Heard. But Heard made an impression on me. He gave me invaluable advice about behaving myself in the department.

Billy told me, "Hey, the only thing I want to tell you, my man, is just keep yourself focused, keep yourself squared away, do what they ask you to do. You'll be all right." He warned me to not challenge them, don't get into any arguments with them, 'cause they can ride you right on out of here. Not too many brothers come out of Hollywood successful.

I felt validated that night. I'd gotten a chance to work with another black police officer, and I found out how to survive within the department. His words meant something, and he had been on some time, he had experience. He'd been around. It wasn't like he was a rookie; he had been on the job a while.

I had other mentors, nonblack mentors like Alan Deal, a captain in my division who took an interest in a young black rookie and pulled me along, developing my people skills and giving me exposure to different assignments. Alan Deal is responsible for where I am today. He's responsible for me having an office here in the Office of Chief of Staff.

Over the years, I feel fortunate to have witnessed and become part of some spectacular events. One detail I was given was when the summer Olympics came to Los Angeles and I was given a detail at the swim-stadium venue—I watched Greg Louganis win his four gold medals. Working the Olympics detail gave me a chance to meet people, work with people, and my name got around, became established with some folks. As a result, I was given opportunities that might not otherwise have been opened up to me.

I always tried to keep my arrogance shoulder-to-shoulder and my ego shoulder-to-shoulder, and never allowed them to get in front of me.

After growing up in Watts, I wanted to give something back to the community, so I worked in the Southeast Division, which is in Watts. I worked undercover in Watts, I worked patrol in Watts. With Darryl Gates acting as chief of police for Los Angeles, his brother, Steven Gates, became captain at Southeast Division. I'm convinced that Captain Gates allowed discrimination and racism to exist in SE Division in 1988.

When one black would leave, another black would take that spot. So, after James Craig left, I took his spot. I was the highest-ranking African-American in the Southeast Division.

In this lead capacity, I got my fifteen minutes of fame. NBC's Tom Brokaw interviewed me for a special that aired on August 17, 1989. It was called *Gangs, Cops and Drugs.*

Brokaw asked me what it was like to grow up in Watts. There were tough times in Los Angeles with gangs, violence, drugs, prostitution, homelessness, crackheads burglarizing homes. It was just a cesspool of social decay.

In the special, I went back to my community and took Brokaw around, showing him where I grew up, what happened to the community, the difference between 1965 and where Watts was as a community in 1989.

People walking the streets with despair, with hopelessness. It was a situation that went from a peaceful community to a community laced with violence and gangs, drugs, crack houses, you name it, murder in the streets, drive-by shootings, young children being gunned down in the streets, innocent bullets, victims of innocent gunfire. As I talked about this with Brokaw, a tear ran down my cheek.

I'm getting all choked up over my own words, Brokaw is asking, what was it like, and what do you feel for these young children today? I went on to tell them to walk in the shoes of this community, to come from poverty, and to try to be able to exist in a society that oftentimes looks at you as a misfit.

The next day, the special aired, August 17, 1989, and the day after, I became a celebrity. I go to work, naturally, and the guys ribbed me real bad 'cause what is a cop doing on television shedding a tear?

But for several weeks, everywhere I went after that, I got phone calls all day long from all across the nation, telling the LAPD, "I want the police officer who was on that TV special."

I'd go into restaurants, and people would ask me for my autograph. What they had seen was a person who was real, and they said, "Man, you touched my heart."

The case that affected me the most happened the day after the special had stopped filming. A little girl was killed in a blazing gun battle out in the Imperial Courts housing projects.

The police couldn't get into the location because they didn't know if the shooting had stopped, and the paramedics were afraid to go in to help her because they would be risking their lives.

Katina Hayley died in a pool of blood, alone. There was no money to bury this little girl. All the officers in the station got together and we collected money to bury the little girl and put a wreath on the casket. And I think that was the moment in my life when I realized how fragile life really is, and how easy it can be taken away.

Today, a sergeant II with LAPD, I work in the public relations department under Deputy Chief Gascon. I have known Gascon since 1973, when I was a police student worker. I credit Gascon with giving me hope and focus in the Los Angeles Police Department. He watched me grow up in the LAPD. He gave me insight, he gave me direction, and he told me that I've got to be a good leader, I've got to stand up for the right things. You have to have character, and that character has to be committed to the right thing. You can't go out and say one thing and do another. You have to be firm, you have to be fair, you have to be honest, you have to be upright.